Your Mind and How to Use it

William Walker Atkinson

DIAMOND BOOKS

www.diamondbooks.in

Publisher : **Diamond Pocket Books (P) Ltd.**
X-30, Okhla Industrial Area,
Phase-II New Delhi-110020
Phone : 011-40712200
E-mail : wecare@diamondbooks.in
Website : www.diamondbook.in
Edition : 2024

Your Mind and How to Use It

By - *William Walker Atkinson*

Preface

In presenting this work, "Your Mind and How to Use It," I aim to offer a comprehensive guide to understanding the capabilities and potentials of the human mind. The principles and practices outlined herein are the culmination of years of study and personal experience in the field of mental science, esoteric philosophy, and self-improvement.

The mind is the most powerful tool at our disposal, yet it remains a largely untapped resource for many. This book seeks to demystify the workings of the mind, offering practical insights into how one can harness its power for personal growth, success, and fulfillment. "Your Mind and How to Use It" is structured to take you step-by-step through the intricacies of mental function and mastery. We will explore the fundamental aspects of consciousness, sub consciousness, and the laws that govern mental processes. By understanding these core principles, you can learn to direct your thoughts, emotions, and actions towards achieving your highest goals.

This book is not just a theoretical exploration but a practical manual. It provides exercises and techniques designed to help you apply what you learn directly to your everyday life. Whether you seek to improve your mental faculties, enhance your personal and professional relationships, or achieve specific ambitions, the guidance offered here is intended to empower you to take control of your mental world.

William Walker Atkinson sets the stage for a deep dive into the vast potentials of the human mind. He emphasizes the incredible power and influence our minds have over our lives, stating that understanding and mastering the mind is key to achieving personal growth, success, and fulfillment.

The book is considered a foundational text in the self-help genre. It explores ideas that are still prevalent today, like the mind-body connection and the power of positive thinking. Atkinson's work helped pave the way for the vast field of self-improvement literature we have today.

About the Author

William Walker Atkinson (1862-1932) was an influential figure in the early 20th-century New Thought movement, an American pioneer in the fields of self-improvement, mental science, and esoteric philosophy. Born in Baltimore, Maryland, Atkinson began his career as a successful lawyer and businessman, but severe health and financial issues led him to explore the powers of the mind and metaphysical healing.

Around the late 19th century, Atkinson discovered the New Thought movement, which emphasized the power of positive thinking, mental visualization, and the law of attraction. His personal experiences with these principles revitalized his health and finances, inspiring him to share his insights through writing. Atkinson's prolific literary career began in earnest around 1900, using numerous pseudonyms, the most notable being Yogi Ramacharaka and Theron Q. Dumont, allowing him to publish a diverse range of works.

He is considered a key figure in shaping modern concepts of the mind-body connection and the Law of Attraction. By day, he was a successful attorney, merchant, and publisher. But his true passion lay in the realm of the mind. Atkinson was a pioneer of the New Thought movement, a philosophical current emphasizing the mind's power to influence our lives. Atkinson's writings covered a broad spectrum of topics, including personal development, mental science, occultism, and Eastern philosophies.

In addition to his books, Atkinson contributed articles to various magazines and edited multiple New Thought periodicals. His clear, practical, and engaging style made complex metaphysical concepts accessible to a wide audience, significantly shaping the self-help genre and New Thought literature.

Atkinson's legacy endures in the ongoing popularity of his works, which continue to inspire readers interested in personal growth, the power of the mind, and esoteric traditions. His contributions laid foundational stones for contemporary self-help literature and the modern understanding of the mind-body connection.

Contents

1

What Is The Mind?

PSYCHOLOGY is generally considered to be the science of mind, although more properly it is the science of mental states—thoughts, feelings, and acts of volition. It was formerly the custom of writers on the subject of psychology to begin by an attempt to define and describe the nature of mind, before proceeding to a consideration of the subject of the various mental spates and activities. But more recent authorities have rebelled against this demand, and have claimed that it is no more reasonable to hold that psychology should be held to an explanation of the ultimate nature of mind than it is that physical science be held to an explanation of the ultimate nature of matter. The attempt to explain the ultimate nature of either is futile—no actual necessity exists for explanation in either case. Physics may explain the phenomena of matter, and psychology the phenomena of mind, without regard to the ultimate nature of the substance of either.

The science of physics has progressed steadily during the past century, notwithstanding the fact that the theories regarding the ultimate nature of matter have been revolutionized during that period. The facts of the phenomena of matter remain, notwithstanding the change of theory regarding the nature of matter itself. Science demands and holds fast to facts, regarding theories as but working hypotheses at the best. Some one has said that "theories are but the bubbles with which the grown-up children of science amuse themselves." Science holds several well-supported, though opposing, theories regarding the nature of electricity, but the *facts* of the phenomena of electricity, and the application thereof, are agreed upon by the disputing theorists. And so it is with psychology; the facts regarding mental states are agreed upon, and methods of developing mental powers are effectively employed, without regard to whether mind is a product of the brain, or the brain merely an organ of the mind. The fact that the brain and nervous system are employed in the phenomena of thought is conceded by all, and that is all that is necessary for a basis for the science of psychology.

Disputes regarding the ultimate nature of mind are now generally passed over to the philosophers and metaphysicians, while psychology devotes its entire attention to studying the laws of mental activities, and to discovering methods of mental development. Even philosophy is beginning to tire of the eternal "why" and is devoting its attention to the "how" phase of things. The pragmatic spirit has invaded the field of philosophy, expressing itself in the words of Prof. William James, who said: "Pragmatism is the attitude of looking away from first things, principles, categories, supposed necessities; and of looking forward toward last things, *fruits, consequences, facts*." Modern psychology is essentially pragmatic in its treatment of the subject of the mind. Leaving to metaphysics the old arguments and disputes regarding the ultimate nature of mind, it bends all its energies upon discovering the laws of mental activities and states, and developing methods whereby the mind may be trained to perform better and more work, to conserve its energies, to concentrate its forces. To modern psychology the mind is *something to be used*, not merely something about which to speculate and theorize. While the metaphysicians deplore this tendency, the practical people of the world rejoice.

Mind Defined

Mind is defined as "the faculty or power whereby thinking creatures, feel, think, and will." This definition is inadequate and circular in nature, but this is unavoidable, for mind can be defined only in its own terms and only by reference to its own processes. Mind, except in reference to its own activities, cannot be defined or conceived. It is known to itself only through its activities. Mind without mental states is a mere abstraction—a word without a corresponding mental image or concept. Sir William Hamilton expressed the matter as clearly as possible, when he said: "What we mean by mind is simply *that which* perceives, thinks, feels, wills, and desires." Without the perceiving, thinking, feeling, willing, and desiring, it is impossible to form a clear conception or mental image of mind; deprived of its phenomena it becomes the merest abstraction.

"Think About That Which Thinks"

Perhaps the simplest method of conveying the idea of the existence and nature of the mind is that attributed to a celebrated German teacher of psychology who was wont to begin his course by bidding his students think of something, his desk, for example. Then he would say, "Now think of *that which thinks about the desk.*" Then, after a pause, he would add, "This thing which thinks about the desk, and about which you are now thinking, is the subject matter of our study of psychology." The professor could not have said more had he lectured for a month.

Professor Gordy has well said on this point: "The mind must either be *that which* thinks, feels, and wills, or it must be the thoughts, feelings, and acts of will of which we are conscious—mental facts, in one word. But what can we know about *that which* thinks, feels, and wills, and what can we find out about it? Where is it? You will probably say, in the brain. But, if you are speaking literally, if you say that it is in the brain, as a pencil is in the pocket, then you must mean that it takes up room, that it occupies space, and that would make it very much like a material thing. In truth, the more carefully you consider it, the more plainly you will see what thinking men have known for a long time—that we do not know and cannot learn anything about the thing which thinks, and feels, and wills. It is beyond the range of human knowledge. The books which define psychology as the science of mind have not a word to say about that which thinks, and feels, and wills. They are entirely taken up with these thoughts and feelings and acts of the will,—mental facts, in a word,—trying to tell us what they are, and to arrange them in classes, and tell us the circumstances or conditions under which they exist. It seems to me that it would be better to define psychology as *the science of the experiences, phenomena, or facts of the mind, soul, or self—of mental facts, in a word.*"

In view of the facts of the case, and following the example of the best of the modern authorities, in this book we shall leave the consideration of the question of the ultimate nature of mind to the metaphysicians, and shall confine ourselves to the *mental facts*, the laws governing them, and the best methods of governing and using them in "the business of life."

The classification and method of development to be followed in this book is as follows:—

I. The mechanism of mental states, *i.e.*, the brain, nervous system, sense organs, etc.

II. The fact of Consciousness and its planes.

III. Mental processes or faculties, *i.e.*, (1) Sensation and Perception; (2) Representation, or Imagination and Memory; (3) Feeling or Emotion; (4) Intellect, or Reason and Understanding; (5) Will or Volition.

Mental states depend upon the physical mechanism for manifestation, whatever may be the ultimate nature of mind. Mental states, whatever their special character, will be found to fit into one of the above five general classes of mental activities.

2
The Mechanism Of Mental States

THE mechanism of mental states—the mental machinery by means of which we feel, think, and will—consists of the brain, nervous system, and the organs of sense. No matter what may be the real nature of mind,—no matter what may be the theory held regarding its activities,—it must be admitted that the mind is dependent upon this mechanism for the manifestation of what we know as mental states. Wonderful as is the mind, it is seen to be dependent upon this physical mechanism for the expression of its activities. And this dependence is not upon the brain alone, but also upon the entire nervous system.

The best authorities agree that the higher and more complex mental states are but an evolution of simple sensation, and that they are dependent upon sensation for their raw material of feeling and thought. Therefore it is proper that we begin by a consideration of the machinery of sensation. This necessitates a previous consideration of the nerves.

The Nerves

The body is traversed by an intricate system of nerves, which has been likened to a great telegraph system. The nerves transmit sensations from the various parts of the body to the great receiving office of the brain. They also serve to transmit the motor impulses from the brain to the various parts of the body, which impulses result in motion of appropriate parts of the body. There are also other nerves with which we have no concern in this book, but which perform certain physiological functions, such as digestion, secretion, excretion, and circulation. Our chief concern, at this point, is with the sensory nerves.

The sensory nerves convey the impressions of the outside world to the brain. The brain is the great central station of the sensory nerves, the latter having countless sending stations in all parts of the body, the "wires" terminating in the skin. When these nervous terminal stations are irritated or excited, they send to the brain messages calling for attention. This is true not only of the nerves of touch or feeling, but also of those concerned with the respective senses of sight, smell, taste, and hearing. In fact, the best authorities hold that all the five senses are but an evolution of the primary sense of touch or feeling.

The Sense of Touch

The nerves of the sense of touch have their ending in the outer covering or skin of the body. They report *contact* with other physical objects. By means of these reports we are aware not only of contact with the outside object, but also of many facts concerning the nature of that object, as for instance, its degree of hardness, roughness, etc., and its temperature. Some of these nerve ends are very sensitive, as, for example, those of the tip of the tongue and finger ends, while others are comparatively lacking in sensitiveness, as, for illustration, those of the back. Certain of these sensory nerves confine themselves to reporting contact and degrees of pressure, while others concern themselves solely with reporting the degrees of temperature of the objects with which their ends come in contact. Some of the latter respond to the higher degrees of heat, while others respond only to the lower degrees of cold. The nerves of certain parts of the body respond more readily and distinctly to temperature than do those of other parts. To illustrate, the nerves of the cheek are quite responsive to heat impressions.

The Sense of Sight

The nerves of the sense of sight terminate in the complex optical apparatus which in popular terminology is known as "the eye." What is known as "the retina" is a very sensitive nervous membrane which lines the inner, back part of the eye, and in which the fibers of the optic nerve terminate. The optical instrument of the eye conveys the focused light vibrations to the nerves of the retina, from which the impulse is transmitted to the brain. But, contrary to the popular notion, the nerves of the eye do not gauge distances, nor form inferences of any kind; that is distinctly the work of the mind. The simple office of the optical nerves consists in reporting color and degrees of intensity of the light waves.

The Sense of Hearing

The nerves of the sense of hearing terminate in the inner part of the ear. The tympanum, or "ear drum," receives the sound vibrations entering the cavities of the ear, and, intensifying and adapting them, it passes them on to the ends of the auditory nerve in the internal ear, which conveys the sensation to the brain. The auditory nerve reports to the brain the degrees of pitch, intensity, quality, and harmony, respectively, of the sound waves reaching the tympanum. As is well known, there are certain vibrations of sound which are too low for the auditory nerve to register, and others too high for it to record, both classes, however, capable of being recorded by scientific instruments. It is also regarded as certain that some of the lower animals are conscious of sound vibrations which are not registered by the human auditory nerves.

The Sense of Smell

The nerves of the sense of smell terminate in the mucous membrane of the nostrils. In order that these nerves report the odor of outside objects, actual contact of minute particles of the object with the mucous membrane of the nostrils is necessary. This is possible only by the passage through the nostrils of air containing these particles; mere nearness to the nostril will not suffice. These particles are for the most part composed of tenuous gases. Certain substances affect the olfactory nerves much more than do others, the difference arising from the chemical composition of the substance. The olfactory nerves convey the report to the brain.

The Sense of Taste

The nerves of the sense of taste terminate in the tongue, or rather in the tiny cells of the tongue which are called "taste buds." Substances taken into the mouth chemically affect these tiny cells, and an impulse is transmitted to the gustatory nerves, which then report the sensation to the brain. The authorities claim that taste sensations may be reduced to five general classes, viz.: sweet, bitter, sour, salty, and "hot."

There are certain nerve centers having important offices in the production and expression of mental states, located in the skull and in the spinal column—the brain and the spinal cord—which we shall consider in the following chapter.

3

The Great Nerve Centers

THE great nerve centers which play an important part in the production and expression of mental states are those of the brain and spinal cord, respectively.

The Spinal Cord

The spinal cord is that cord or rope of nerve substance which is inclosed in the spinal column or "backbone." It leaves the lower part of the skull and extends downward in the interior of the spinal column for about eighteen inches. It is continuous with the brain, however, and it is difficult to determine where one begins and the other ends. It is composed of a mass of gray matter surrounded by a covering of white matter. From the spinal cord, along its length, emerge thirty-one pairs of spinal nerves which branch out to each side of the body and connect with the various smaller nerves, extending to all parts of the system. The spinal cord is the great central cable of the nervous telegraphic system, and any injury to or obstruction of it cripples or paralyzes those portions of the body the nerves of which enter the spinal cord below the seat of the injury or obstruction. Injuries or obstructions of this kind not only inhibit the sensory reports from the affected area, but also inhibit the motor impulses from the brain which are intended to move the limbs or parts of the body.

The Ganglia or "Tiny Brains"

What are known as ganglia, or tiny bunches of nerve cells, are found in various parts of the nervous system, including the spinal nerves. These groups of nerve cells are sometimes called "little brains," and perform quite important offices in the mechanism of thought and action. The spinal ganglia receive sensory reports, and issue motor impulses, in many cases, without troubling the central brain regarding the matter. These activities are known as "reflex nervous action."

Reflex Action

What is known as reflex nervous action is one of the most wonderful of the activities of the nervous and mental mechanism, and the knowledge thereof usually comes as a surprise to the average person, for he is generally under the impression that these activities are possible only to the central brain. It is a fact that not only is the central brain really a trinity of three brains, but that, in addition to these, every one has a great number of "little brains" distributed over his nervous system, any and all of which are capable of receiving sensory reports and also of sending forth motor impulses. It is quite worth while for one to become acquainted with this wonderful form of neuro-mental activity.

A cinder enters the eye, the report reaches a ganglion, a motor impulse is sent forth, and the eyelid closes. The same result ensues if an object approaches the eye but without actually entering it. In either case the person is not conscious of the sensation and motor impulse until the latter has been accomplished. This is reflex action. The instinctive movement of the tickled foot is another instance. The jerking away of the hand burnt by the lighted end of the cigar, or pricked by the point of the pin, is another instance. The involuntary activities, and those known as unconscious activities, result from reflex action.

More than this, it is a fact that many activities originally voluntary become what is known as "acquired reflexes," or "motor habits," by means of certain nervous centers acquiring the habit of sending forth certain motor impulses in response to certain sensory reports. The familiar movements of our lives are largely performed in this way, as, for instance, walking, using knife and fork, operating typewriters, machines of all kinds, writing, etc. The squirming of a decapitated snake, the muscular movements of a decapitated frog, and the violent struggles, fluttering, and leaps of the decapitated fowl, are instances of reflex action. Medical reports indicate that in cases of decapitation even man may manifest similar reflex action in some cases. Thus we may see that we may *feel* and *will* by means of our "little brains" as well as by the central brain or brains. Whatever mind may be, it is certain that in these processes it employs other portions of the nervous system than the central brain.

The Three Brains

What is known as the brain of man is really a trinity of three brains, known respectively as (1) the *medulla oblongata*, (2) the *cerebellum*, and (3) the *cerebrum*. If one wishes to limit the mental activity to conscious intellectual effort, then and then only is he correct in considering the cerebrum or large brain as "the brain."

The Medulla Oblongata.—The medulla oblongata is an enlargement of the spinal cord at the base of the brain. Its office is that of controlling the involuntary activities of the body, such as respiration, circulation, assimilation, etc. In a broad sense, its activities may be said to be of the nature of highly developed and complex reflex activities. It manifests chiefly through the sympathetic nervous system which controls the vital functions. It does not need to call on the large brain in these matters, ordinarily, and is able to perform its tasks without the plane of ordinary consciousness.

The Cerebellum.—The cerebellum, also known as "the little brain," lies just above the medulla oblongata, and just below the rear portion of the cerebrum or great brain. It combines the nature of a purely reflex center on the one hand, with that of "habit mind" on the other. In short, it fills a place between the activities of the cerebrum and the medulla oblongata, having some of the characteristics of each. It is the organ of a number of important acquired reflexes, such as walking, and many other familiar muscular movements, which have first been consciously acquired and then become habitual. The skilled skater, bicyclist, typist, or machinist depends upon the cerebellum for the ease and certainty with which he performs his movements "without thinking of them." One may be said never to have thoroughly acquired a set of muscular movements such as we have mentioned, until the cerebellum has taken over the task and relieved the cerebrum of the conscious effort. One's technique is never perfected until the cerebellum assumes control and direction of the necessary movements and the impulses are sent forth from below the plane of ordinary consciousness.

The Cerebrum.—The cerebrum, or "great brain" (which is regarded as "the brain" by the average person), is situated in the upper portion of the skull, and occupies by far the larger portion of the cavity of the skull. It is divided into two great divisions or hemispheres. The best of the modern authorities are agreed that the cerebrum has zones or areas of specialized functioning, some of which receive the sensory reports of the nerves and organs of sense, while others send forth the motor impulses which result in voluntary physical action. Many of these areas or zones have been located by science, while others remain as yet unlocated. The probability is that in time science will succeed in correctly locating the area or zone of each and every class of sensation and motor impulse.

The Cortex

The area of thought, memory, and imagination has not been clearly located, except that these mental states are believed to have their seat in the *cortex* or outer thin rind of gray brain matter which envelopes and covers the mass of brain substance. It is, moreover, considered probable that the higher processes of reasoning are performed in or by the cortex of the frontal lobes. The cortex of a person of average intelligence, if spread out on a flat surface, measures about four square feet. The higher the degree of intelligence possessed by a lower animal or human being, as a rule, the deeper and more numerous are the folds or convolutions of the cortex, and the finer its structure. It may be stated as a general rule, with but very few exceptions, that the higher the degree of intelligence in a lower animal or human being, the greater is the area of its cortex in proportion to the size of the brain. The cortex, it must be remembered, is folded into deep furrows or convolutions, the brain in shape, divisions, and convolutions resembling the inner portion of an English walnut. The interior of the two hemispheres of the cerebrum is composed largely of connective nerves which doubtless serve to produce and maintain the unity of function of the mental processes.

While physiological psychology has performed great work in discovering brain-centers and explaining much of the mechanism of mental processes, it has but touched the most elementary and simple of the mental processes. The higher processes have so far defied analysis or explanation in the terms of physiology.

4
Consciousness

THE fact of consciousness is the great mystery of psychology. It is difficult even to define the term, although every person of average intelligence understands what is sought to be conveyed by it. Webster defines it as "knowledge of one's own existence, sensations, mental operations, etc.; immediate knowledge or perception of any object, state, or sensation; being aware; being sensible of." Another authority defines the term as "the state of being aware of one's sensations; the power, faculty, or mental state of being aware of one's own existence, condition at the moment, thoughts, feelings, and actions." Halleck's definition is: "That indefinable characteristic of mental states which causes us to be aware of them."

It will be seen that the idea of "awareness" is the essence of the idea of consciousness. But, at the last, we are compelled to acknowledge that it is impossible to closely define consciousness, for it is something so entirely unique and different from anything else that we have no other terms at all synonymous to it. We can define it only in its own terms, as will be seen by reference to the definitions above given. And it is equally impossible to clearly account for its appearance and being. Huxley has well said: "How it is that anything so remarkable as a state of consciousness comes about by the result of irritating nervous tissue, is just as unaccountable as the appearance of the jinnee when Aladdin rubbed his lamp." All that we can ever know regarding the nature of consciousness must be learned from turning the consciousness in ourselves back upon itself—by focusing consciousness upon its own mental operations by means of introspection. By turning inward the conscious gaze we may perceive the flow of the stream of thought from its rise from the subconscious regions of the mind to its final disappearance in the same region.

It is a common error to suppose that we are directly conscious of objects outside of ourselves. This is impossible, for there is no direct knowledge of such outside objects. We are conscious merely of our sensations of, or mental images of, the outside objects. All that it is possible for us to be directly conscious of are our own mental experiences or states. We cannot be directly conscious of anything outside of our own minds. We are not directly conscious of the tree which we *see*; we are directly conscious merely of the sensation of the nerves arising from the impact of the light waves carrying the image of the tree. We are not directly conscious of the tree when we touch it and perceive its character in that way; we are directly conscious merely of the sensation reported by the nerves in the finger tips which have come in contact with the tree. We are directly conscious even of our own bodies only in the same way. It is necessary for the mind to experience that of which it may become conscious. We are conscious only of (1) that which our mind is experiencing at this moment, or (2) that which it has experienced in the past, and which is being re-experienced this moment by the process of the memory, or which is being re-combined or re-arranged this moment by the imagination.

Subconscious Planes

But it must not be thought that every mental state or mental fact is in the field of consciousness. This error has been exploded for many years. The fact is now recognized that the field of consciousness is a very narrow and limited one, and that the great field of mental activity lies outside of its narrow limits. Beyond and outside of the narrow field of consciousness lies the great subconscious storehouse of memory in which are stored the experiences of the past, to be drawn again into the field of consciousness by an effort of the will in the act of recollection, or by association in ordinary remembrance. In that great region, also, the mind manifests many of its activities and performs much of its work. In that great region are evolved the emotions and feelings which play such an important part in our lives, and which often manifest a vague disturbing unrest long before they rise to the plane of consciousness. In that great region are produced the ideas, feelings, and conceptions which arise to the plane of consciousness and manifest that which men call "genius."

On the subconscious plane the imagination does much of its work, and startles its owner by presenting him with the accomplished result in the field of consciousness. In the subconscious field is performed that peculiar process of mental mastication, digestion, and assimilation with which all brain workers are familiar, and which absorbs the raw mental material given it, separates, digests, and assimilates it, and re-presents it to the conscious faculties sometime after as a transformed substance. It has been estimated that at least eighty-five per cent. of our mental activities are performed below or outside of the field of consciousness. The psychology of to-day is paying much attention to this formerly neglected great area or areas of the mind. The psychology of to-morrow will pay still greater attention to it.

The best of the modern authorities agree that in the great field of subconscious mentation is to be found the explanation of much that is unexplainable otherwise. In fact, it is probable that before long consciousness will be regarded as a mere *focusing of attention* upon mental states, and the objects of consciousness merely as that portion of the contents of the mind in the field of mental vision created by such focusing.

5
Attention

INTIMATELY connected with the object of consciousness is that process of the mind which we call "attention." Attention is generally defined as "the application of the mind to a mental state." It is often referred to as "concentrated consciousness," but others have ventured the somewhat daring conjecture that consciousness itself is rather the result of attention, instead of the latter being an incident of consciousness. We shall not attempt to discuss this question here, except to state that consciousness depends very materially upon the degree of attention bestowed upon its object. The authorities place great importance upon the intelligent direction of the attention, and hold that without this the higher forms of knowledge are impossible.

It is the common belief that we feel, see, hear, taste, or smell whenever objects affecting those senses come in contact with the organs of sense governing them. But this is only a partial truth. The real truth is that we become conscious of the report of these senses only when the attention is directed toward the sensation, voluntarily or involuntarily. That is to say, that in many cases although the sense nerves and organs report a disturbance, the mind does not become consciously aware of the report unless the attention is directed toward it either by an act of will or else by reflex action. For instance, the clock may strike loudly, and yet we may not be conscious of the fact, for we are concentrating our attention upon a book; or we may eat the choicest food without tasting it, for we are listening intently to the conversation of our charming neighbor. We may fail to perceive some startling occurrence happening under our very eyes, for we are buried in deep thought concerning something far removed from the present scene. There are many cases on record showing that one may be so interested in speaking, thinking, or acting that he will not experience pain that would otherwise be intolerable. Writers have forgotten their pain in the concentrated interest bestowed upon their work; mothers have failed to feel pain when their infants required urgent attention; orators have been so carried away by their own eloquence that they have failed to feel the pricking of the pin by means of which their friends have sought to attract their attention. Not only perception and feeling depend largely upon attention, but the processes of reasoning, memory, and even of will, depend upon attention for much of their manifestation.

Psychologists divide attention into two general classes, viz.: (1) voluntary attention and (2) involuntary attention.

Voluntary attention is attention directed by the will to some object of our own more or less deliberate selection. It requires a distinct effort of the will in order to focus the attention in this way, and many persons are scarcely aware of its existence, so seldom do they manifest it. Voluntary attention is the result of training and practice, and marks the man of strong will, concentration, and character. Some authorities go so far as to say that much of that which is commonly called "will power" is really but a developed form of voluntary attention, the man of "strong will" holding before him the one idea which he wishes to realize.

Involuntary attention, often called "reflex attention," is attention called forth by a nervous response to some sense stimulus. This is the common form of attention, and is but the same form which is so strongly manifested by children whose attention is caught by every new object, but which cannot be held for any length of time by a familiar or uninteresting one.

It is of the utmost importance that one should cultivate his power of voluntary attention. Not only is the will power strengthened and developed in this way, but every mental faculty is developed by reason thereof. The training of the voluntary attention is the first step in mental development.

Training the Attention

That the voluntary attention may be deliberately trained and developed is a fact which many of the world's greatest men have proved for themselves. There is only one way to train and develop any mental power of faculty—and that is *by practice and use*. By practice, interest may be given to objects previously uninteresting, and thus the use of the attention develops the interest which further holds it. Interest is the natural road over which attention travels easily, but interest itself may be induced by concentrated attention. By studying and examining an object, the attention brings to light many new and novel features regarding the thing, and these produce a new interest which in turn attracts further and continued attention.

There is no royal road to the development of voluntary attention. The only true method is *work, practice, and use*. You must practice on uninteresting things, the primary interest being your desire to develop the power of voluntary attention. But as you begin to attend to the uninteresting thing you will become interested in the task for its own sake. Take some object and "place your mind upon it." Think of its nature, where it came from, its use, its associations, its probable future, of things related to it, etc., etc. Keep the attention firmly upon it, and shut out all outside ideas. Then, after a little practice of this kind, lay aside the object for the time being, and take it up again the next day, endeavoring to discover new points of interest in it. The main thing to be sought is *to hold the thing in your mind*, and this can be done only by *discovering features of interest in it*. The interest-loving attention may rebel at this task at first, and will seek to wander from the path into the green pastures which are found on each side thereof. But you must bring the mind back to the task, again and again.

After a time the mind will become accustomed to the drill, and will even begin to enjoy it. Give it some variety by occasionally changing the objects of examination. The object need not always be something to be looked at. Instead, select some subject in history or literature, and "run it down," endeavoring to bring to light all the facts relating to it that are possible to you. *Anything* may be used as the subject or object of your inquiry; but what is chosen must be held in the field of conscious attention firmly and fixedly. The habit once acquired, you will find the practice most fascinating. You will invent new subjects or objects of inquiry, investigation, and thought, which in themselves will well repay you for your work and time. But never lose sight of the main point—the development of the power of voluntary attention.

In studying the methods of developing and training the voluntary attention, the student should remember that *any* exercise which develops the will, will result in developing the attention; and, likewise, any exercise which develops the voluntary attention will tend to strengthen the will. The will and attention are so closely bound together that what affects one also influences the other. This fact should be borne in mind, and the exercises and practices based upon it.

In practicing concentration of voluntary attention, it should be remembered that concentrating consists not only of *focusing* the attention upon a given object or subject, but also of the *shutting out* of impressions from other objects or subjects. Some authorities advise that the student endeavor to listen to one voice among many, or one instrument among the many of a band or orchestra. Others advise the practice of concentrating on the reading of a book in a room filled by persons engaged in conversation, and similar exercises. Whatever aids in *narrowing the circle* of attention at a given moment tends to develop the power of voluntary attention.

The study of mathematics and logic is also held to be an excellent practice in concentration of voluntary attention, inasmuch as these studies require close concentration and attention. Attention is also developed by any study or practice which demands *analysis* of a whole into its parts, and then the *synthesis* or building up of a whole from its scattered parts. Each of the senses should play a part in the exercises, and in addition to this the mind should be trained to concentrate upon some one idea held within itself—some mental image or abstract idea existing independently of any object of immediate sense report.

6
Perception

IT is a common mistake that we *perceive* everything that is reported to the mind by the senses. As a matter of fact we perceive but a very small portion of the reports of the senses. There are thousands of sights reported by our eyes, sounds reported by our ears, smells reported by our nostrils, and contacts reported by our nerves of touch, every day of our lives, but which are not *perceived* or *observed* by the mind. We perceive and observe only when the attention, reflex or voluntary, is directed to the report of the senses, and when the mind interprets the report. While perception depends upon the reports of the senses for its raw material, it depends entirely upon the application of the mind for its complete manifestation.

The student usually experiences great difficulty in distinguishing between *sensation* and *perception*. A sensation is a simple report of the senses, which is received in consciousness. Perception is the *thought* arising from the *feeling* of the sensation. Perception usually combines several sensations into one thought or percept. By sensation the mind *feels*; by perception it *knows* that it feels, and recognizes the object causing the sensation. Sensation merely brings a report from outside objects, while perception identifies the report with the object which caused it. Perception *interprets* the reports of sensation. Sensation reports a flash of light from above; perception interprets the light as starlight, or moonlight, or sunlight, or as the flash of a meteor. Sensation reports a sharp, pricking, painful contact; perception interprets it as the prick of a pin. Sensation reports a red spot on a green background; perception interprets it as a berry on a bush.

Moreover, while we may perceive a simple single sensation, our perceptions are usually of a group of sensations. Perception is usually employed in grouping sensations and identifying them with the object or objects causing them. In its identification it draws upon whatever memory of past experiences the mind may possess. Memory, imagination, feeling, and thought are called into play, to some extent, in every clear perception. The infant has but feeble perception, but as it gains experience it begins to manifest perceptions and form percepts. Sensations resemble the letters of the alphabet, and perception the forming of words and sentences from the letters. Thus *c*, *a*, and *t* symbolize sensations, while the word "cat," formed from them, symbolizes the perception of the object.

It is held that all knowledge begins with sensation; that the mental history of the race or individual begins with its first sensation. But, while this is admitted, it must be remembered that sensation simply provides the simple, elementary, raw material of thought. The first process of *actual thought*, or knowledge, begins with perception. From our percepts all of our higher concepts and ideas are formed. Perception depends upon association of the sensation with other sensations previously experienced; it is based upon experience. The greater the experience, the greater is the possibility of perception, all else being equal.

When perception begins, the mind loses sight of the sensation in itself, for it identifies it as a quality of the thing producing it. The sensation of light is thought of as a quality of the star; the pricking sensation is thought of as a quality of the pin or chestnut bur; the sensation of odor is thought of as a quality of the rose. In the case of the rose, the several sensations of sight, touch, and smell, in their impression of the qualities of color, shape, softness, and perfume, are grouped together in the percept of the complete object of the flower.

A *percept* is "that which is perceived; the object of the act of perception." The percept, of course, is a mental state corresponding with its outside object. It is a combination of several sensations which are regarded as the qualities of the outside object, to which are combined the memories of past experiences, ideas, feelings, and thoughts. A percept, then, while the simplest form of thought, is seen to be a mental state. The formation of a percept consists of three gradual stages, viz.: (1) The attention forms definite conscious sensations from indefinite nervous reports; (2) the mind interprets these definite conscious sensations and attributes them to the outside object causing them; (3) the related sensations are grouped together, their unity perceived, and they are regarded as qualities of the outside object.

The plain distinction between a sensation and a percept may be fixed in the mind by remembering the following: *A sensation is a feeling; a percept is a simple thought identifying one or more sensations.* A sensation is merely the conscious recognition of an excitation of a nerve end; a percept results from a distinct mental process regarding the sensation.

Developing Perception

It is of the utmost importance that we develop and train our powers of perception. For our education depends very materially upon our perceptive power. What matters it to us if the outside world be filled with manifold objects, if we do not perceive them to exist? Upon perception depends the material of our mental world. Many persons go through the world without perceiving even the most obvious facts. Their eyes and ears are perfect instruments, their nerves convey accurate reports, but the perceptive faculties of the mind fail to observe and interpret the report of the senses. They see and hear distinctly, but the reports of the senses are not observed or noted by them; they mean nothing to them. One may see many things, and yet *observe* but few. It is not upon what we see or hear that our stock of knowledge depends, so much as it does upon what we perceive, notice, or observe.

Not only is one's stock of practical knowledge largely based upon developed perception, but one's success also depends materially upon the same faculties. In business and professional life the successful man is usually he who has developed perceptive powers; he who has learned to perceive, observe, and note. The man who perceives and takes mental notes of what occurs in his world is the man who is apt to know things when such knowledge is needed. In this age of "book education" we find that the young people are not nearly so observant as are those children who had to depend upon the powers of perception for their knowledge. The young Arab or Indian will observe more in an hour than the civilized child will in a day. To live in a world of books tends, in many cases, to weaken the powers of observation and perception.

Perception may be developed by practice. Begin by taking notice of the things seen and heard in your usual walks. Keep wide open the eyes of the mind. Notice the faces of people, their walk, their characteristics. Look for interesting and odd things, and you will see them. Do not go through life in a daydream, but keep a sharp lookout for things of interest and value. The most familiar things will repay you for the time and work of examining them in detail, and the practice gained by such tasks will prove valuable in your development of perception.

An authority remarks that very few persons, even those living in the country, know whether a cow's ears are above, below, behind, or in front of her horns; nor whether cats descend trees head first or tail first. Very few persons can distinguish between the leaves of the various kinds of familiar trees in their neighborhood. Comparatively few persons are able to describe the house in which they live, at least beyond the most general features—the details are unknown.

Houdin, the French conjurer, was able to pass by a shop window and perceive every article in it, and then repeat what he had seen. But he acquired this skill only by constant and gradual practice. He himself decried his skill and claimed that it was as nothing compared to that of the fashionable woman who can pass another woman on the street and "take in" her entire attire, from head to foot, at one glance, and "be able to describe not only the fashion and quality of the stuffs, but also say if the lace be real or only machine made." A former president of Yale is said to have been able to glance at a book and read a quarter of a page at one time.

Any study or occupation which requires *analysis* will develop the power of perception. Consequently, if we will analyze the things we see, resolving them into their parts or elements, we will likewise develop the perceptive faculties. It is a good exercise to examine some small object and endeavor to discover as many separate points of perception as possible, noting them on a sheet of paper. The most familiar object, if carefully examined, will yield rich returns.

If two persons will enter into a contest of this kind, the spirit of rivalry and competition will quicken the powers of observation. Those who have had the patience and perseverance to systematically practice exercises of this kind, report that they notice a steady improvement from the very start. But even if one does not feel inclined to practice in this way, it will be found possible *to begin to take notice* of the details of things one sees, the expression of persons' faces, the details of their dress, their tone of voice, the quality of the goods we handle, and *the little things especially*. Perception, like attention, follows interest; but, likewise, interest may be created in things by observing their details, peculiarities, and characteristics.

The best knowledge gained by one is that resulting from his own personal perception. There is a nearness and trueness about that which one *knows* in this way which is lacking in that which he merely *believes* because he has read or heard it. One can make such knowledge a part of himself. Not only is one's knowledge dependent upon what he perceives, but his very character also results from the character of his percepts. The influence of environment is great—and what is environment but things perceived about one? It is not so much what lies outside of one, as what part of it gets *inside* of one by perception. By directing his attention to desirable objects, and perceiving as much of them as is possible, one really builds his own character at will.

The world needs good "perceivers" in all the walks of life. It finds a shortage of them, and is demanding them loudly, being willing to pay a good price for their services. The person who can voluntarily perceive and observe the details of any profession, business, or trade will go far in that vocation. The education of children should take the faculty of perception into active consideration. The kindergarten has taken some steps in this direction, but there is much more to be done.

7
Memory

PSYCHOLOGISTS class as "representative mental processes" those known as memory and imagination, respectively. The term "representation" is used in psychology to indicate the processes of re-presentation or presenting again to consciousness that which has formerly been presented to it but which afterward passed from its field. As Hamilton says: "The general capability of knowledge necessarily requires that, besides the power of evoking out of unconsciousness one portion of our retained knowledge in preference to another, we possess the faculty of representing in consciousness what is thus evoked."

Memory is the primary representative faculty or power of the mind. Imagination depends upon memory for its material, as we shall see when we consider that faculty. Every mental process which involves the remembrance, recollection, or representation of a sensation, perception, mental image, thought, or idea previously experienced must depend upon memory for its material. Memory is the great storehouse of the mind in which are placed the records of previous mental experiences. It is a part of the great subconscious field of mental activity, and the greater part of its work is performed below the plane of consciousness. It is only when its results are passed into the field of consciousness that we are aware of its existence. We know memory only by its works. Of its nature we know but little, although certain of its principal laws and principles have been discovered.

It was formerly customary to class memory with the various faculties of the mind, but later psychology no longer so considers it. Memory is now regarded as a power of the general mind, manifesting in connection with every faculty of the mind. It is now regarded as belonging to the great subconscious field of mentation, and its explanation must be sought there. It is utterly unexplainable otherwise.

The importance of memory cannot be overestimated. Not only does a man's character and education depend chiefly upon it, but his very mental being is bound up with it. If there were no memory, man would never progress mentally beyond the mental state of the newborn babe. He would never be able to profit by experience. He would never be able to form clear perceptions. He would never be able to reason or form judgments. The processes of thought depend for material upon the memory of past experiences; this material lacking, there can be no thought.

Memory has two important general functions, viz.: (1) The *retention* of impressions and experiences; and (2) the *reproduction* of the impressions and experiences so retained.

It was formerly held that the memory retained only a portion of the impressions and experiences originally noted by it. But the present theory is that it retains every impression and experience which is noted by it. It is true that many of these impressions are never reproduced in consciousness, but experiments tend to prove, nevertheless, that the records are still in the memory and that appropriate and sufficiently strong stimuli will bring them into the field of consciousness. The phenomena of somnambulism, dreams, hysteria, delirium, approach of death, etc., show that the subconscious mind has an immense accumulation of apparently forgotten facts, which unusual stimuli will serve to recall.

The power of the memory to reproduce the retained impressions and experiences is variously called remembrance, recollection, or memory. This power varies materially in various individuals, but it is an axiom of psychology that the memory of any person may be developed and trained by practice. The ability to recall depends to a great extent upon the clearness and depth of the original impression, which in turn depends upon the degree of attention given to it at the time of its occurrence. Recollection is also greatly aided by the law of association, or the principle whereby one mental fact is linked to another. The more facts to which a given fact is linked, the greater the ease by which it is recalled or remembered. Recollection is also greatly assisted by use and exercise. Like the fingers, the memory cells of the brain become expert and efficient by use and exercise, or stiff and inefficient by lack of the same.

In addition to the phases of retention and reproduction, there are two important phases of memory, viz.: (3) Recognition of the reproduced impression or experience; and (4) localization of the impression, or its reference to a more or less definite time and place.

The recognition of the recalled impression is quite important. It is not enough that the impression be retained and recalled. If we are not able to recognize the recalled impression as having been experienced before, the recollection will be of but little use to us in our thought processes; the purposes of thought demand that we shall be able to identify the recalled impression with the original one. Recognition is really re-cognition—re-knowing. Recognition is akin to perception. The mind becomes conscious of the recalled impression just as it becomes conscious of the sensation. It then recognizes the relation of the recalled impression to the original one just as it realizes the relation of the sensation to its object.

The localization of the recalled and recognized impression is also important. Even if we recognize the recalled impression, it will be of comparatively little use to us unless we are able to locate it as having happened yesterday, last week, last month, last year, ten years ago, or at some time in the past; and as having happened in our office, house, or in such-and-such a place in the street, or in some distant place. Without the power of localization we should be unable to connect and associate the remembered fact with the time, place, and persons with which it should be placed to be of use and value to us in our thought processes.

Retention

The retention of a mental impression in the memory depends very materially upon the clearness and depth of the original impression. And this clearness and depth, as we have previously stated, depend upon the degree of attention bestowed upon the original impression. Attention, then, is the important factor in the forming and recording of impressions. The rule is: *Slight attention, faint record*; *marked attention, clear and deep record*. To fix this fact in the mind, the student may think of the retentive and reproductive phases of memory as a phonographic record. The receiving diaphragm of the phonograph represents the sense organs, and the recording needle represents the *attention*. The needle makes the record on the cylinder deep or faint according to the condition of the needle. A loud sound may be recorded but faintly, if the needle is not properly adjusted. And, further, it must be remembered that the strength of the reproduction depends almost entirely upon the clearness and depth of the original impression on the cylinder; as is the record, so is the reproduction. It will be well for the student to carry this symbol of the phonograph in his mind; it will aid him in developing his powers of memory.

In this connection we should remember that attention depends largely upon interest. Therefore we would naturally expect to find that we remember interesting things far more readily than those which lack interest. This supposition is borne out in actual experience. This accounts for the fact that every one remembers a certain class of things better than he does others. One remembers faces, another dates, another spoken conversation, another written words, and so on. It will be found, as a rule, that each person is interested in the class of things which he most easily remembers. The artist easily remembers faces and details of faces, or scenery and details thereof. The musician easily recalls passages or bars of music, often of a most complicated nature. The speculator easily recalls the quotations of his favorite stocks. The racing man recalls without difficulty the "odds" posted on a certain horse on a certain day, or the details of a race which was run many years ago. The moral is: *Arouse and induce an interest in the things which you wish to remember.* This interest may be aroused by studying the things in question, as we have suggested in a preceding chapter.

Visualization in Memory

Many of the best authorities hold that original impressions may be made clear and deep, and the process of reproduction accordingly rendered more efficient, by the practice of *visualizing* the thing to be remembered. By visualizing is meant the formation of a *mental image* of the thing in the imagination. If you wish to remember the appearance of anything, look at it closely, with attention, and then turning away from it endeavor to reproduce its appearance as a mental picture in the mind. If this is done, a particularly clear impression will be made in the memory, and when you recall the thing you will find that you will also recall the clear mental image of it. Of course the greater the number of details observed and included in the original mental image, the greater the remembered detail.

Perception in Memory

Not only is attention necessary in forming clear memory records, but careful perception is also important. Without clear perception there is a lack of detail in the retained record, and the element of association is lacking. It is not enough to merely remember the thing itself; we should also remember *what* it is, and all about it. The practice of the methods of developing perception, given in a preceding lesson, will tend to develop and train the retentive, reproductive, recognitive, and locative powers of the memory. The rule is: *The greater the degree of perception accorded a thing, the greater the detail of the retained impression, and the greater the ease of the recollection.*

Understanding and Memory

Another important point in acquiring impressions in memory is this: That the better the understanding of the subject or object, the clearer the impressions regarding it, and the clearer the recollection of it. This fact is proved by experiment and experience.

A subject which will be remembered only with difficulty under ordinary circumstances will be easily remembered if it is fully explained to the person, and accompanied by a few familiar illustrations or examples. It is very difficult to remember a meaningless string of words, while a sentence which conveys a clear meaning may be memorized easily. If we understand what a thing is for, its uses and employment, we remember it far more easily than if we lack this understanding. Elbringhaus, who conducted a number of experiments along this line, reports that he could memorize a stanza of poetry in about one tenth the time required to memorize the same amount of nonsense syllables.

Gordy states that he once asked a capable student of the Johns Hopkins University to give him an account of a lecture to which he had just listened. "I cannot do it," replied the student; "it was not logical." The rule is: The more one knows about a certain thing, the more easily is that thing remembered. This is a point worth noting.

8
Memory—Continued

THE subject of memory cannot be touched upon intelligently without a consideration of the Law of Association, one of the important psychological principles.

The Law of Association

What is known in psychology as the Law of Association is based on the fact that *no idea exists in the mind except in association with other ideas.* This is not generally recognized, and the majority of persons will dispute the law at first thought. But the existence and appearance of ideas in the mind are governed by a mental law as invariable and constant as the physical law of gravitation. Every idea has associations with other ideas. Ideas travel in groups, and one group is associated with another group, and so on, until in the end every idea in one's mind is associated directly or indirectly with every other idea. Theoretically, at least, it would be possible to begin with one idea in the mind of a person, and then gradually unwind his entire stock of ideas like the yarn on the ball. Our thoughts proceed according to this law. We sit down in a "brown study" and proceed from one subject to another, until we are unable to remember any connection between the first thought and the last. But each step of the reverie was connected with the one preceding and the one succeeding it. It is interesting to trace back these connections. Poe based one of his celebrated detective stories on this law. The reverie may be broken into by a sudden impression from outside, and we will then proceed from that impression, connecting it with something else already in our experience, and starting a new chain of sequence.

Often we fail to trace the associations governing our ideas, but the chain is there nevertheless. One may think of a past scene or experience without any apparent cause. A little thought will show that something seen, or a few notes of a song floating to the ears, or the fragrance of a flower, has supplied the connecting link between the past and the present. A suggestion of mignonette will recall some past event in which the perfume played a part; some one's handkerchief, perhaps, carried the same odor. Or an old familiar tune reminds one of some one, something, or some place in the past. A familiar feature in the countenance of a passer-by will start one thinking of some one else who had that kind of a mouth, that shaped nose, or that expression of the eye—and away he will be off in a sequence of remembered experiences. Often the starting idea, or the connecting links, may appear but dimly in consciousness; but rest assured they are always there. In fact, we frequently accept this law, unconsciously and without realizing its actual existence. For instance, one makes a remark, and at once we wonder, "How did he come to think of that?" and, if we are shrewd, we may discover what was in his mind before he spoke.

There are two general classes of association of ideas in memory, viz.: (1) Association of contiguity, and (2) logical association.

Association of contiguity is that form of association depending upon the previous association in time or space of ideas which have been impressed on the mind. For instance, if you met Mr. and Mrs. Wetterhorn and were introduced to them one after the other, thereafter you will naturally remember Mr. W. when you think of Mrs. W., and vice versa. You will naturally remember Napoleon when you think of Wellington, or Benedict Arnold when you think of Major André, for the same reason. You will also naturally remember *b* and *c* when you think of *a*. Likewise, you will think of abstract time when you think of abstract space, of thunder when you think of lightning, of colic when you recall green apples, of love making and moonlight nights when you think of college days. In the same way we remember things which occurred just before or just after the event in our mind at the moment; of things near in space to the thing of which we are thinking.

Logical association depends upon the relation of likeness or difference between several things thought of. Things thus associated may have never come into the mind at the same previous time, nor are they necessarily connected in time and space. One may think of a book, and then proceed by association to think of another book by the same author, or of another author treating of the same subject. Or he may think of a book directly opposed to the first, the relation of distinct difference causing the associated idea. Logical association depends upon *inner relations*, and not upon the outer relations of time and space. This *innerness* of relation between things not connected in space or time is discovered only by experience and education. The educated man realizes many points of relationship between things that are thought by the uneducated man to be totally unrelated. Wisdom and knowledge consist largely in the recognition of relations between things.

Association in Memory

It follows from a consideration of the Law of Association that when one wishes to impress a thing upon the memory he should, as an authority says, "Multiply associations; entangle the fact you wish to remember in a net of as many associations as possible, especially those that are logical." Hence the advice to place your facts in groups and classes in the memory. As Blackie says: "Nothing helps the mind so much as order and classification. Classes are always few, individuals many; to know the class well is to know what is most essential in the character of the individual, and what burdens the memory least to retain."

Repetition in Memory

Another important principle of memory is that the impressions acquire depth and clearness by repetition. Repeat a line of poetry once, and you may remember it; repeat it again, and your chances of remembering it are greatly increased; repeat it a sufficient number of times, and you cannot escape remembering it. The illustration of the phonograph record will help you to understand the reason of this. The rule is: *Constant repetition deepens memory impressions; frequent reviewing and recalling what has been memorized tends to keep the records clear and clean, beside deepening the impression at each review.*

General Rules of Memory

The following general rules will be of service to the student who wishes to develop his memory:—

Making Impressions.

(1) Bestow attention.

(2) Cultivate interest.

(3) Manifest perception.

(4) Cultivate understanding.

(5) Form associations.

(6) Repeat and review.

Recalling Impressions.

(1) Endeavor to get hold of the loose end of association, and then unwind your memory ball of yarn.

(2) When you recall an impression, send it back with energy to deepen the impression, and attach it to as many new associations as possible.

(3) Practice a little memorizing and recalling each day, if only a line of verse. The memory improves by practice, and deteriorates by neglect and disuse.

(4) Demand good service of your memory, and it will learn to respond. Learn to trust it, and it will rise to the occasion. How can you expect your memory to give good service when you continually abuse it and tell every one of "the wretched memory I have; I can never remember anything"? Your memory is very apt to accept your statements as truth; our mental faculties have an annoying habit of taking us at our word in these matters. Tell your memory what you expect it to do; then trust it and refrain from abusing it and giving it a bad name.

Final Advice

Finally, remember this rule: You get out of your memory only that which you place in it. Place in it good, clear, deep impressions, and it will reproduce good, clear, strong recollections. Think of your memory as a phonographic record, and take care that you place the right kind of impressions upon it. In memory you reap that which you have sown. You must give to the memory before you can receive from it. Of one thing you may rest assured, namely, that unless you take sufficient interest in the things to be remembered, you will find that the memory will not take sufficient interest in them to remember them. Memory demands interest before it will take interest in the task. It demands attention before it will give attention. It demands understanding before it will give understanding. It demands association before it will respond to association. It demands repetition before it will repeat. The memory is a splendid instrument, but it stands on its dignity and asserts its rights. It belongs to the old dispensation—it demands compensation and believes in giving only in equal measure to what it receives. Our advice is to get acquainted with your memory, and make friends with it. Treat it well and it will serve you well. But neglect it, and it will turn its back on you.

9
Imagination

THE imagination belongs to the general class of mental processes called the representative faculties, by which is meant the processes in which there are re-presented, or presented again, to consciousness impressions previously presented to it.

As we have indicated elsewhere, the imagination is dependent upon memory for its materials—its records of previous impressions. But imagination is more than mere memory or recollection of these previously experienced and recorded impressions. There is, in addition to the re-presentation and recollection, a process of arranging the recalled impressions into new forms and new combinations. The imagination not only gathers together the old impressions, but also *creates* new combinations and forms from the material so gathered.

Psychology gives us many hairsplitting definitions and distinctions between simple reproductive imagination and memory, but these distinctions are technical and as a rule perplexing to the average student. In truth, there is very little, if any, difference between simple reproductive imagination and memory, although when the imagination indulges in constructive activity a new feature enters into the process which is absent in pure memory operations. In simple reproductive imagination there is simply the formation of the mental image of some previous experience—the reproduction of a previous mental image. This differs very little from memory, except that the recalled image is clearer and stronger. In the same way in ordinary memory, in the manifestation of recollection, there is often the same clear, strong mental image that is produced in reproductive imagination. The two mental processes blend into each other so closely that it is practically impossible to draw the line between them, in spite of the technical differences urged by the psychologists. Of course the mere remembrance of a person who presents himself to one is nearer to pure memory than to imagination, for the process is that of recognition. But the memory or remembrance of the same person when he is absent from sight is practically that of reproductive imagination. Memory, in its stage of recognition, exists in the child mind before reproductive imagination is manifested. The latter, therefore, is regarded as a higher mental process.

But still higher in the scale is that which is known as *constructive imagination*. This form of imagination appears at a later period of child mentation, and is regarded as a later evolution of mental processes of the race. Gordy makes the following distinction between the two phases of imagination: "The difference between reproductive imagination and constructive imagination is that the images resulting from reproductive imagination are *copies of past experience*, while those resulting from constructive imagination are not.

* * *

To learn whether any particular image, or combination of images, is the product of reproductive or constructive imagination, all we have to do is to learn whether or not it is a copy of a past experience. Our memories, of course, are defective, and we may be uncertain on that account; but apart from that, we need be in no doubt whatever."

Many persons hearing for the first time the statement of psychologists that the imaginative faculties can re-present and re-produce or re-combine only the images which have previously been impressed upon the mind, are apt to object that they can, and frequently do, image things which they have not previously experienced. But can they and do they? Is it not true that what they believe to be original creations of the imagination are merely *new combinations* of original impressions? For instance, no one ever saw a unicorn, and yet some one originally imagined its form. But a little thought will show that the image of the unicorn is merely that of an animal having the head, neck, and body of a horse, with the beard of a goat, the legs of a buck, the tail of a lion, and a long, tapering horn, spirally twisted, in the middle of the forehead. Each of the several parts of the unicorn exists in some living animal, although the unicorn, composed of all of these parts, is non-existent outside of fable. In the same way the centaur is composed of the body, legs, and tail of the horse and the trunk, head, and arms of a man. The satyr has the head, body, and arms of a man, with the horns, legs, and hoofs of a goat. The mermaid has the head, arms, and trunk of a woman, joined at the waist to the body and tail of a fish. The mythological "devil" has the head, body, and arms of a man, with the horns, legs, and cloven foot of the lower animal, and a peculiar tail composed of that of some animal but tipped with a spearhead. Each of these characteristics is composed of familiar images of experience. The imagination may occupy itself for a lifetime turning out impossible animals of this kind, but every part thereof will be found to correspond to something existent in nature, and experienced by the mind of the person creating the strange beast.

In the same way the imagination may picture a familiar person or thing acting in an unaccustomed manner, the latter having no basis in fact so far as the individual person or thing is concerned, but being warranted by some experience concerning other persons or things. For instance, one may easily form the image of a dog swimming under water like a fish, or climbing a tree like a cat. Likewise, one may form a mental image of a learned, bewigged High Chancellor, or a venerable Archbishop of Canterbury, dressed like a clown, standing on his head, balancing a colored football on his feet, sticking his tongue in his cheek and winking at the audience. In the same way one may imagine a railroad running across a barren desert, or a steep mountain, upon which there is not as yet a rail laid. The bridge across a river may be imaged in the same way. In fact, this is the way that everything is mentally created, constructed, or invented—the old materials being combined in a new way, and arranged in a new fashion. Some psychologists go so far as to say that no mental image of memory is an exact reproduction of the original impression; that there are always changes due to the unconscious operation of the constructive imagination.

The constructive imagination is able to "tear things to pieces" in search for material, as well as to "join things together" in its work of building. The importance of the imagination in all the processes of intellectual thought is great. Without imagination man could not reason or manifest any intellectual process. It is impossible to consider the subject of thought without first regarding the processes of imagination. And yet it is common to hear persons speak of the imagination as if it were a faculty of mere fancy, useless and without place in the practical world of thought.

Developing the Imagination

The imagination is capable of development and training. The general rules for development of the imagination are practically those which we have stated in connection with the development of the memory. There is the same necessity for plenty of material; for the formation of clear and deep impressions and clear-cut mental images; the same necessity for repeated impression, and the frequent use and employment of the faculty. The practice of visualization, of course, strengthens the power of the imagination as it does that of the memory, the two powers being intimately related. The imagination may be strengthened and trained by deliberately recalling previous impressions and then combining them into new relations. The materials of memory may be torn apart and then re-combined and re-grouped. In the same way one may enter into the feelings and thoughts of other persons by imagining one's self in their place and endeavoring to act out in imagination the life of such persons. In this way one may build up a much fuller and broader conception of human nature and human motives.

In this place, also, we should caution the student against the common waste of the powers of the imagination, and the dissipation of its powers in idle fancies and daydreams. Many persons misuse their imagination in this way and not only weaken its power for effective work but also waste their time and energy. Daydreams are notoriously unfit for the real, practical work of life.

Imagination and Ideals

And, finally, the student should remember that in the category of the imaginative powers must be placed that phase of mental activity which has so much to do with the making or marring of one's life—the formation of ideals. Our ideals are the patterns after which we shape our life. According to the nature of our ideals is the character of the life we lead.

Our ideals are the supports of that which we call *character.*

It is a truth, old as the race, and now being perceived most clearly by thinkers, that indeed "as a man thinketh in his heart so is he." The influence of our ideals is perceived to affect not only our character but also our place and degree of success in life. We grow to be that of which we have held ideals. If we create an ideal, either of general qualities or else these qualities as manifested by some person living or dead, and keep that ideal ever before us, we cannot help developing traits and qualities corresponding to those of our ideal. Careful thought will show that character depends greatly upon the nature of our ideals; therefore we see the effect of the imagination in character building.

Moreover, our imagination has an important bearing on our actions. Many a man has committed an imprudent or immoral act which he would not have done had he been possessed of an imagination which showed him the probable results of the action. In the same way many men have been inspired to great deeds and achievements by reason of their imagination picturing to them the possible results of certain action. The "big things" in all walks of life have been performed by men who had sufficient imagination to picture the possibilities of certain courses or plans. The railroads, bridges, telegraph lines, cable lines, and other works of man are the results of the imagination of some men. The good fairy godmother always provides a vivid and lively imagination among the gifts she bestows upon her beloved godchildren. Well did the old philosopher pray to the gods: "And, with all, give unto me a clear and active imagination."

The dramatic values of life depend upon the quality of the imagination. Life without imagination is mechanical and dreary. Imagination may increase the susceptibility to pain, but it pays for this by increasing the capacity for joy and happiness. The pig has but little imagination,—little pain and little joy,—but who envies the pig? The person with a clear and active imagination is in a measure a creator of his world, or at least a re-creator. He takes an active part in the creative activities of the universe, instead of being a mere pawn pushed here and there in the game of life.

Again, the divine gift of sympathy and understanding depends materially upon the possession of a good imagination. One can never understand the pain or problems of another unless he first can imagine himself in the place of the other. Imagination is at the very heart of sympathy. One may be possessed of great capacity for feeling, but owing to his lack of imagination may never have this feeling called into action. The person who would sympathize with others must first learn to understand them and feel their emotions. This he can do only if he has the proper degree of imagination. Those who reach the heart of the people must first be reached by the feelings of the people. And this is possible only to him whose imagination enables him to picture himself in the same condition as others, and thus awaken his latent feelings and sympathies and understanding. Thus it is seen that the imagination touches not only our intellectual life but also our emotional nature. Imagination is the very life of the soul.

10
The Feelings

IN thinking of the mind and its activities we are accustomed to the general idea that the mental processes are chiefly those of intellect, reason, thought. But, as a fact, the greater part of the mental activities are those concerned with feeling and emotion. The intellect is the youngest child of the mind, and while making its presence strenuously known in the manner of all youngest children so that one is perhaps justified in regarding it as "the whole thing" in the family, nevertheless it really plays but a comparatively small part in the general work of the mental family. The activities of the "feeling" side of life greatly outnumber those of the "thinking" side, are far stronger in their influence and effect, as a rule, and, in fact, so color the intellectual processes, unconsciously, as to constitute their distinctive quality except in the case of a very few advanced thinkers.

But there is a difference between "feeling" and "emotion," as the terms are employed in psychology. The former is the simple phase, the latter the complex. Generally speaking, the resemblance or difference is akin to that existing between sensation and perception, as explained in a previous chapter. Beginning with the simple, in order later on to reach the complex, we shall now consider that which is known as simple "feeling."

The term "feeling," as used in this connection in psychology, has been defined as "the simple *agreeable* or *disagreeable* side of any mental state." These agreeable or disagreeable sides of mental states are quite distinct from the act of knowing, which accompanies them. One may perceive and thus "know" that another is speaking to him and be fully aware of the words being used and of their meaning. Ordinarily, and so far as pure thought processes are concerned, this would complete the mental state. But we must reckon on the feeling side as well as on the thinking side of the mental state. Accordingly we find that the knowledge of the words of the other person and the meaning thereof results in a mental state agreeable or disagreeable. In the same way the reading of the words of a book, the hearing of a song, or a sight or scene perceived, may result in a more or less strong feeling, agreeable or disagreeable. This sense of agreeable or disagreeable consciousness is the essential characteristic of what we call "feeling."

It is very difficult to explain feeling except in its own terms. We know very well what we mean, or what another means, when it is said that we or he "*feels* sad," or has "a joyous feeling," or "a feeling of interest." And yet we shall find it very hard to explain the mental state except in terms of feeling itself. Our knowledge depends entirely upon our previous experience of the feeling. As an authority says: "If we have never felt pleasure, pain, fear, or sorrow, a quarto volume cannot make us understand what such a mental state is." Every mental state is not distinguished by strong feeling. There are certain mental states which are concerned chiefly with intellectual effort, and in which all trace of feeling seems to be absent, unless, as some have claimed, the "feeling" of interest or the lack of same is a faint form of the feeling of pleasure or pain. Habit may dull the feeling of a mental state until it is apparently neutral, but there is generally a faint feeling of like or dislike still left.

The elementary forms of feeling are closely allied with those of simple sensation. But experiments have revealed that there is a distinction in consciousness. It has been discovered that one is often conscious of the "touch" of a heated object before he is of the feeling or pain resulting from it. Psychologists have pointed out another distinction, namely: When we experience a sensation we are accustomed to refer it to the outside thing which is the object of it, as when we touch the heated object; but when we experience a feeling we instinctively refer it to ourself, as when the heated object gives us pain. As an authority has said: "My feelings belong to me; but my sensations seem to belong to the object which caused them."

Another proof of the difference and distinction between sensation and feeling is the fact that the same sensation will produce different feelings in different persons experiencing the former, even at the same time. For instance, the same sight will cause one person to feel elated, and the other depressed; the same words will produce a feeling of joy in one, and a feeling of sorrow in another. The same sensation will produce different feelings in the same person at different times. An authority well says: "You drop your purse, and you see it lying on the ground as you stoop to pick it up, with no feeling either of pleasure or pain. But if you see it after you have lost it and have hunted for it a long time in vain, you have a pronounced feeling of pleasure."

There is a vast range of degree and kind in feeling. Gordy says: "All forms of pleasure and pain are called feelings. Between the pleasure which comes from eating a peach and that which results from solving a difficult problem, or learning good news of a friend, or thinking of the progress of civilization—between the pain that results from a cut in the hand and that which results from the failure of a long-cherished plan or the death of a friend—there is a long distance. But the one group are all pleasures; the other all pains. And, whatever the source of the pleasure or pain, it is alike feeling."

There are many different kinds of feelings. Some arise from sensations of physical comfort or discomfort; others from purely physiological conditions; others from the satisfaction of accustomed tastes, or the dissatisfaction arising from the stimulation of unaccustomed tastes; others from the presence or absence of comfort; others from the presence or absence of things or persons for whom we have an affection or liking. Over-indulgence often transforms the feeling of pleasure into that of pain; and, likewise, habit and practice may cause us to experience a pleasurable feeling from that which formerly inspired feeling of an opposite kind. Feelings also differ in degree; that is to say, some things cause us to experience pleasurable feelings of a greater intensity than do others, and some cause us to experience painful feelings of a greater intensity than do others. These degrees of intensity depend more or less upon the habit or experience of the individual. As a general rule, feelings may be classified into (1) those arising from physical sensations, and (2) those arising from ideas.

The feelings depending upon physical sensations arise either from inherited tendencies and inclinations or from acquired habits and experience. It is an axiom of the evolutionary school that any physical activity that has been a habit of the race, long continued, becomes an instinctive pleasure-giving activity in the individual. For instance, the race for many generations was compelled to hunt, fish, travel, swim, etc., in order to maintain existence. The result is that we, the descendants, are apt to find pleasure in the same activities as sport, games, exercise, etc. Many of our tendencies and feelings are inherited in this way. To these we have added many acquired habits of physical activity, which follow the same rule, *i.e.*, that habit and practice impart more or less pleasurable feeling. We find more pleasure in doing those things which we can do easily or quite well than in the opposite kind of things.

The feelings depending upon ideas may also arise from inheritance. Many of our mental tendencies and inclinations have come down to us from the past. There are certain feelings that are born in one, without a doubt; that is to say, there is a great capacity for such feelings which will be transformed into manifestation upon the presentation of the proper stimulus. Other mental feelings depend upon our individual past experience, association, or suggestions from others—upon our past environment, in fact. The ideals of those around us will cause us to experience pleasure or pain, as the case may be, under certain circumstances; the force of suggestion along these lines is very strong indeed. Not only do we experience feelings in response to present sensations, but the recollection of some previous experience will also arouse feeling. In fact, feelings of this kind are closely bound up with memory and imagination. Persons of vivid imagination are apt to feel far more than others. They suffer more, and enjoy more. Our sympathies, which depend largely upon our imaginative power, are the cause of many of our feelings of this kind.

Many of the facts which we generally ascribe to feeling are really a part of the phenomena of emotion, the latter being the more complex phase of feeling. For the purposes of this consideration we have regarded simple feeling as the raw material of emotion, the relation being compared to that existing between sensation and perception. In our consideration of emotion we shall see the fuller manifestation of feeling, and its more complex expressions.

11
The Emotions

AS we have seen in the preceding lessons, an emotion is the more complex phase of feeling. As a rule an emotion arises from a number of feelings. Moreover, it is of a higher order of mental activity. As we have seen, a feeling may arise either from a physical sensation or from an idea. Emotion, however, as a rule, is dependent upon *an idea* for its expression, and always upon an idea for its direction and its continuance. Feeling, of course, is the elemental spirit of all emotional states, and, as an authority has said, is the thread upon which the emotional states are strung.

Halleck says: "When representative ideas appear, the feeling in combination with them produces emotion. After the waters of the Missouri combine with another stream, they receive a different name, although they flow toward the gulf in as great volume as before. Suppose we liken the feeling due to sensation to the Missouri River; the train of representative ideas to the Mississippi before its junction with the Missouri. Emotion may then be likened to the Mississippi *after* its junction—after feeling has combined with representative ideas. The emotional stream will not be broader and deeper than before. This analogy is employed only to make the distinction clearer. The student must remember that mental powers are never actually as distinct as two rivers before their union.

* * *

The student must beware of thinking that we have done with feeling when we consider emotion. Just as the waters of the Missouri flow on until they reach the gulf, so does feeling run through every emotional state." In the above analogy the term "representative ideas," of course, means the ideas of memory and imagination as explained in previous chapters.

There is a close relation between emotion and the physical expression thereof—a peculiar mutual action and reaction between the mental state and the physical action accompanying it. Psychologists are divided regarding this relation. One school holds that the physical expression follows and results from the mental state. For instance, we hear or see something, and thereupon experience the feeling or emotion of anger. This emotional feeling reacts upon the body and causes an increased heart beat, a tight closing of the lips, a frown and lowered eyebrows, and clinched fists. Or we may perceive something which causes the feeling or emotion of fear, which reacts upon the body and produces pallor, raising of the hair, dropping of the jaw, opening of the eyelids, trembling of the legs, etc. According to this school, and the popular idea, the mental state precedes and causes the physical expression.

But another school of psychology, of which the late Prof. William James is a leading authority, holds that the physical expression precedes and causes the mental state. For instance, in the cases above cited, the perception of the anger-causing or fear-causing sight first causes a reflex action upon the muscles, according to inherited race habits of expression. This muscular expression and activity, in turn, is held to react upon the mind and to cause the feeling or emotion of anger or fear, as the case may be. Professor James, in some of his works, makes a forcible argument in support of this theory, and his opinions have influenced the scientific thought of the day upon this subject. Others, however, have sought to combat his theory by equally forcible argument, and the subject is still under lively and spirited discussion in psychological circles.

Without taking sides in the above controversy, many psychologists proceed upon the hypothesis that there is a mutual action and reaction between emotional mental states and the appropriate physical expression thereof, each in a measure being the cause of the other, and each likewise being the effect of the other. For instance, in the cases above cited, the perception of the anger-producing or fear-producing sight causes, almost or quite simultaneously, the emotional mental state of anger or fear, as the case may be, and the physical expression thereof. Then rapidly ensues a series of mental and physical reactions. The mental state acts upon the physical expression and intensifies it. The physical expression in turn reacts upon the mental state and induces a more intense degree of the emotional feeling. And so on, until the mental state and physical expression reach their highest point and then begin to subside from exhaustion of energy. This middle-ground conception meets all the requirements of the facts, and is probably more nearly correct than either extreme theory.

Darwin in his classic work, "The Expression of the Emotions in Man and Animals," has thrown a great light on the subject of the expression of emotion in physical motions. The Florentine scientist, Paolo Mantegazza, added to Darwin's work with ideas of his own and countless examples drawn from his own experience and observation. The work of François Delsarte, the founder of the school of expression which bears his name, is also a most valuable addition to the thought on this subject. The subject of the relation and reaction between emotional feeling and physical expression is a most fascinating one, and one in which we may expect interesting and valuable discoveries during the next twenty years.

The relation and reaction above mentioned are interesting not only from the viewpoint of theory but also because of their practicable application in emotional development and training. It is an established truth of psychology that each physical expression of an emotional state serves to intensify the latter; it is pouring oil on the fire. Likewise, it is equally true that the repression of the physical expression of an emotion tends to restrain and inhibit the emotion itself.

Halleck says: "If we watch a person growing angry, we shall see the emotion increase as he talks loud, frowns deeply, clinches his fist, and gesticulates wildly. Each expression of his passion is reflected back upon the original anger and adds fuel to the fire. If he resolutely inhibits the muscular expressions of his anger, it will not attain great intensity, and it will soon die a quiet death.

* * *

Not without reason are those persons called cold blooded who habitually restrain as far as possible the expression of their emotion; who never frown or throw any feeling into their tones, even when a wrong inflicted upon some one demands aggressive measures. There is here no wave of bodily expression to flow back and augment the emotional state."

In this connection we call your attention to the familiar and oft-quoted passage from the works of Prof. William James: "Refuse to express a passion and it dies. Count ten before venting your anger and its occasion seems ridiculous. Whistling to keep up courage is no mere figure of speech. On the other hand, sit all day in a moping posture, sigh and reply to everything with a dismal voice, and your melancholy lingers. There is no more valuable precept in moral education than this, as all who have experience know: If we wish to conquer undesirable emotional tendencies in ourselves, we must assiduously, and in the first instance cold-bloodedly, go through the outward movements of those contrary dispositions which we prefer to cultivate. Smooth the brow, brighten the eye, contract the dorsal rather than the ventral aspect of the frame, and speak in a major key, and your heart must be frigid indeed if it does not gradually thaw."

Along the same lines Halleck says: "Actors have frequently testified to the fact that emotion will arise if they go through the appropriate muscular movements. In talking to a character on the stage, if they clinch the fists and frown, they often find themselves becoming really angry; if they start with counterfeit laughter, they find themselves growing cheerful. A German professor says that he cannot walk with a schoolgirl's mincing step and air without feeling frivolous."

The wise student will acquire a great control over his emotional nature if he will re-read and study the above statements and quotations until he has grasped their spirit and essence. In those few lines he is given a philosophy of self-control and self-mastery that will be worth much to him if he will but apply it in practice. Patience, perseverance, practice, and will are required, but the reward is great. Even to those who have not the persistency to apply this truth fully, there will be a partial reward if they will use it to the extent of restraining so far as possible any undue physical expression of undesirable emotional excitement.

Some writers seem to regard capacity for great emotional excitement and expression as a mark of a rich and full character or noble soul. This is far from being true. While it is a fact that the cultivation of certain emotions tends to create a noble character and a full life, it is equally true that the tendency to "gush" and indulge in hysterical or sentimental excesses is a mark of an ill-controlled nature and a weak, rather than strong, character. Moreover, it is a fact that excess in emotional excitement and expression tends toward the dissipation of the finer and nobler feelings which otherwise would seek an outlet in actual doing and practical action. In the language of the old Scotch engineer in the story, they are like the old locomotive which "spends sae much steam at the whustle that she hae nane left to gae by."

Emotional excitement and expression are largely dependent upon habit and indulgence, although there is a great difference, of course, in the emotional nature and tendencies of various persons. Emotions, like physical actions or intellectual processes, become habitual by repetition. And habit renders all physical or mental actions easy of repetition. Each time one manifests anger, the deeper the mental path is made, and the easier it is to travel that path the next time. In the same way each time that anger is conquered and inhibited, the easier will it be to restrain it the next time. In the same way desirable habits of emotion and expression may be formed.

Another point in the cultivation, training, and restraint of the emotions is that which has to do with the control of the ideas which we allow to come into the mind. Ideative habits may be formed—*are* formed, in fact, by the majority of persons. We may cultivate the habit of looking on the bright side of things; of looking for the best in those we meet; of expecting the best things instead of the worst. By resolutely refusing to give welcome to ideas calculated to arouse certain emotions, feelings, passions, desires, sentiments, or similar mental states, we may do much to prevent the arousing of the emotion itself. Emotions usually are called forth by some idea, and if we shut out the idea we may prevent the emotional feeling from appearing. In this connection the universal rule of psychology may be applied: *A mental state may be inhibited or restrained by turning the attention to the opposite mental state.*

The control of the attention is really the control of every mental state.

We may use the will in the direction of the control of the attention—the development and direction of voluntary attention—and thus actually control every phase of mental activity. The will is nearest to the ego, or central being of man, and the attention is the chief tool and instrument of the will. This fact cannot be repeated too often.

If it is impressed upon the mind it will prove to be useful and valuable in many emergencies of mental life. He who controls his attention controls his mind, and in controlling his mind controls himself.

12
The Instinctive Emotions

MANY attempts to classify the emotions have been made by the psychologists, but the best authorities hold that beyond the purpose of ordinary convenience in considering the subject *any* classification is scientifically useless by reason of its incompleteness. As James cleverly puts it: "Any classification of the emotions is seen to be as true and as natural as any other, if it only serves some purpose." The difficulty attending the attempted classification arises from the fact that every emotion is more or less complex, and is made up of various feelings and shades of emotional excitement. Each emotion blends into others. Just as a few elements of matter may be grouped into hundreds of thousands of combinations, so the elements of feeling may be grouped into thousands of shades of emotion. It is said that the two elements of carbon and hydrogen form combinations resulting in five thousand varieties of material substance, "from anthracite to marsh gas, from black coke to colorless naphtha." The same thing may be said of the emotional combinations formed from two principal elements of feeling. Moreover, the close distinction between sensation and feeling on the one hand, and between feeling and emotion on the other, serves to further complicate the task.

For the purposes of our consideration, let us divide the emotions into five general classes, as follows: (1) Instinctive emotions, (2) social emotions, (3) religious emotions, (4) æsthetic emotions, (5) intellectual emotions. We shall now consider each of the above five classes in turn.

The Instinctive Emotions

Instinct is defined as "unconscious, involuntary, or unreasoning prompting to any action," or "the natural unreasoning impulse by which an animal is guided to the performance of any action, without thought of improving the method." An authority says: "Instinct is a natural impulse leading animals, even prior to all experience, to perform certain actions tending to the welfare of the individual or the perpetuation of the species, apparently without understanding the object at which they may be supposed to aim, or deliberating as to the best methods to employ. In many cases, as in the construction of the cells of the bee, there is a perfection about the result which reasoning man could not have equaled, except by an application of the higher mathematics to direct the operations carried out. Mr. Darwin considers that animals, in time past as now, have varied in their mental qualities, and that those variations are inherited. Instincts also vary slightly in a state of nature. This being so, natural selection can ultimately bring them to a high degree of perfection."

It was formerly the fashion to ascribe instinct in the lower animals, and in man, to something akin to "innate ideas" implanted in each species and thereafter continued by inheritance. But the application of the idea of evolution to the science of psychology has resulted in brushing away these old ideas. To-day it holds that that which we call "instinct" is the result of gradual development in the course of evolution, the accumulated experience of the race being stored away in the race memory, each individual adding a little thereto by his acquired habits and experiences. Psychologists now hold that the lower forms of these race tendencies are closely akin to purely reflex actions, and the higher forms, which are known as "instinctive emotions," are phenomena of the subconscious mind resulting from race memory and race experience.

Clodd says: "Instinct is the higher form of reflex action. The salmon migrates from sea to river; the bird makes its nest or migrates from one zone to another by an unvarying route, even leaving its young behind to perish; the bee builds its six-sided cell; the spider spins its web; the chick breaks its way through the shell, balances itself, and picks up grains of corn; the newborn babe sucks its mother's breast—all in virtue of like acts on the part of their ancestors, which, arising in the needs of the creature, and gradually becoming automatic, have not varied during long ages, the tendency to repeat them being transmitted within the germ from which insect, fish, bird, and man have severally sprung."

Schneider says: "It is a fact that men, especially in childhood, fear to go into a dark cavern, or a gloomy wood. This feeling of fear arises, to be sure, partly from the fact that we easily suspect that dangerous beasts may lurk in these localities—a suspicion due to stories we have heard and read. But, on the other hand, it is quite sure that this fear at a certain perception is also directly inherited. Children who have been carefully guarded from all ghost stories are nevertheless terrified and cry if led into a dark place, especially if sounds are made there. Even an adult can easily observe that an uncomfortable timidity steals over him in a lonely wood at night, although he may have the fixed conviction that not the slightest danger is near. This feeling of fear occurs in many men even in their own houses after dark, although it is much stronger in a dark cavern or forest. The fact of such instinctive fear is easily explicable when we consider that our savage ancestors through immemorable generations were accustomed to meet with dangerous beasts in caverns, especially bears, and were for the most part attacked by such beasts during the night and in the woods, and that thus an inseparable association between the perceptions of darkness, caverns, woods, and fear took place, and was inherited."

James says: "Nothing is commoner than the remark that man differs from lower creatures by the almost total absence of instincts, and the assumption of their work in him by reason.

* * *

We may confidently say that however uncertain man's reactions upon his environment may sometimes seem in comparison with those of the lower mammals, the uncertainty is probably not due to their possession of any principles of action which he lacks. *On the contrary, man possesses all the impulses that they have, and a great many more besides.*

* * *

High places cause fear of a peculiarly sickening sort, though here again individuals differ. The utterly blind instinctive character of the motor impulses here is shown by the fact that they are almost always entirely unreasonable, but that reason is powerless to suppress them.

* * *

Certain ideas of supernatural agency, associated with real circumstances, produce a peculiar kind of horror. This horror is probably explicable as the result of a combination of simple horrors. To bring the ghostly terror to its maximum, many unusual elements of the dreadful must combine, such as loneliness, darkness, inexplicable sounds, especially of a dismal character, moving pictures half discerned (or, if discerned, of dreadful aspect), and a vertiginous baffling of the expectation.

* * *

In view of the fact that cadaveric, reptilian, and underground horrors play so specific and constant a part in many nightmares and forms of delirium, it seems not altogether unwise to ask whether these forms of dreadful circumstance may not at a former period have been more normal objects of the environment than now. The evolutionist ought to have no difficulty in explaining these terrors, and the scenery that provokes them, as relapses into the consciousness of the cave men, a consciousness usually overlaid in us by experiences of a more recent date."

Instinctive emotion manifests as an impulse arising from the dim recesses of the feeling or emotional nature—an incentive toward a dimly conscious end. It differs from the almost purely automatic nature of certain forms of reflex process, for its beginning is a feeling arising from the subconscious regions, which strives to excite an activity of conscious volition. The feeling is from the subconscious, but the activity is conscious. The end may not be perceived in consciousness, or at least is but dimly perceived, but the action leading to the end is in full consciousness. Instinct is seen to have its origin in the past experiences of the race, transmitted by heredity and preserved in the race memory. It has for its object the preservation of the individual and of the species. Its end is often something far removed in time from the moment, or the welfare of the species rather than that of the individual; for instance, the caterpillar providing for its future states, or the bird building its nest, or the bees building cells and providing honey for their successors, for very few bees live to partake of the honey which they have gathered and stored—they are animated by "the spirit of the hive."

The most elementary forms of the instinctive emotions are those which have to do with the preservation of the individual, his comfort, and personal physical welfare. This class of emotions comprises what are generally known as purely "selfish" feelings, having little or no concern for the welfare of others.

In this class we find the emotional feelings which have to do with the satisfaction of hunger and thirst, the securing of comfortable quarters and warm clothing, and the spirit of combat and strife arising from the desire to obtain these. These elemental feelings had their birth early in the history of life, and indeed life itself depended very materially upon them for its preservation and continuance. It was necessary for the primitive living thing to be "selfish."

When man appeared, only those survived who manifested these feelings strongly; the others were pushed to the wall and perished. Even in our civilization the man below the average in this class of feelings will find it difficult to survive.

13
The Passions

ARISING from the most elemental instinctive emotions, we find what may be termed "the passions." By the term "passion" is meant those strong feelings in which the elemental selfish instincts are manifested in relation to other persons, either in the phase of attraction or repulsion. In this class we find the elementary phases of love, and the feelings of hate, anger, jealousy, revenge, etc. This class of emotions usually manifests violently, as compared with the other emotions. The passions generally arise from self-preservation, race preservation and reproduction, self-interest, self-aggrandizement, etc., and may be regarded as a more complex phase of the elemental instinctive emotions. The elemental instinctive emotions of self-preservation and self-comfort cause the individual to experience and manifest the passional emotions of desire for combat, anger, hate, revenge, etc., while the instinctive emotions leading to reproduction and continuance of the race give rise to the passional emotions of sexual love, jealousy, etc. The desire to attract the other sex increases ambition, vanity, love of display, and other feelings.

It is only when this class of emotions blends with the higher emotions that the passions become purified and refined. But it must not be forgotten that these emotions were very necessary for the welfare of the race in the early stage of its evolution, and that they still play an active part in human life, under the greater or less restraint imposed by civilized society. Nor should it be forgotten that from these emotions have evolved the highest love of one human being for another. From instinctive sexual love and the "racial instinct" have developed the higher affection of man for woman, and woman for man, in all their beautiful manifestations—and the love of the parent for the child, and the love of the child for the parent. The first manifestation of altruism arises in the love of the living creature for its mate, and in the love of the parents for their offspring. In certain forms of life where the association of the sexes is merely for the moment, and is not followed by protection, mutual aid, and companionship, there is found an absence of mutual affection of any kind, the only feeling being an elemental reproductive instinct bringing the male and female together for the moment—an almost purely reflex activity. In the same way, in the cases of certain animals (the rattlesnake, for instance) in which the young are able to protect themselves from birth, there is seen a total absence of parental affection or the return thereof. Human love between the sexes, in its higher and lower degrees, is a natural evolution from passional emotion of a low order, due to the growth of social, ethical, moral, and æsthetic emotion arising from the necessities of the increasing complexity and development of human life.

The simpler forms of passional emotion are almost entirely instinctive in their manifestation. Indeed, in many cases, there appears to be but little more than a high form of reflex nervous action. The following words of William James give us an interesting view of this fact of life: "The cat runs after the mouse, runs or shows fight before the dog, avoids falling from walls and trees, shuns fire and water, not because he has any notion either of life or of death or of self-preservation. He acts in each case separately and simply because he cannot help it; being so framed that when that particular running thing called a mouse appears in his field of vision, he *must* pursue; that when that particular barking and obstreperous thing called a dog appears there, he *must* retire if at a distance, and scratch if close by; that he *must* withdraw his feet from water, and his face from flame, etc.

* * *

Now, why do the various animals do what seem to us such strange things in the presence of such outlandish stimuli? Why does the hen, for instance, submit herself to the tedium of incubating such a fearfully uninteresting set of objects as a nestful of eggs, unless she have some sort of prophetic inkling of the result? The only answer is *ad hominem*. We can only interpret the instinct of brutes by what we know of instincts in ourselves. Why do men always lie down, when they can, on soft beds rather than on soft floors? Why do they sit around a stove on a cold day? Why, in a room, do they place themselves, ninety-nine times out of a hundred, with their faces toward its middle rather than to the wall? Why does the maiden interest the youth so much that everything about her seems more important and significant than anything else in the world? Nothing more can be said than that these are human ways, and that every creature likes its own ways, and takes to following them as a matter of course. Science may come and consider these ways, and find that most of them are useful. But it is not for the sake of their utility that they are followed, but because at the moment of following them we feel that it is the only appropriate and natural thing to do. Not one man in a million, when taking his dinner, ever thinks of its utility. He eats because the food tastes good, and makes him want more. If you should ask him *why* he wants to eat more of what tastes like that, instead of revering you as a philosopher he will probably laugh at you for a fool."

James continues: "It takes, in short, what Berkeley called a mind debauched by learning to carry the process of making the natural seem strange, so far as to ask the *why* of any instinctive human act. To the metaphysician alone can such questions arise as: Why do we smile when pleased and not scowl? Why are we unable to talk to a crowd as to a single friend? Why does a particular maiden turn our wits upside down? The common man can only say, '*Of course* we smile, *of course* our heart palpitates at the sight of the crowd, *of course* we love the maiden—that beautiful soul clad in that perfect form, so palpably and flagrantly made from all eternity to be loved!' And so, probably, does each animal feel about the particular things it tends to do in the presence of particular objects. They, too, are *a priori* syntheses. To the lion it is the lioness which is made to be loved; to the bear, the she bear. To the broody hen the notion would seem monstrous that there should be a creature in the world to whom a nestful of eggs was not the utterly fascinating, precious, and never-to-be-too-much-sat-upon object which it is to her. Thus we may be sure that however mysterious some animals' instincts may appear to us, our instincts will appear no less mysterious to them. And we may conclude that, to the animal which obeys it, every impulse and every step of that instinct shines with its own sufficient light, and seems at the moment the only externally right and proper thing to do. It may be done for its own sake exclusively."

One has very little need, as a rule, to develop the passional emotions. Instinct has taken pretty good care that we shall have our share of this class of feelings. But there is a need to train, restrain, govern, and control these emotions, for the conditions which brought about their original being have changed. Our social conventions require that we should subordinate these passional feelings, to some extent at least. Society insists that we must restrict our love impulses to certain limits and to certain quarters, and that we subdue our anger and hate, except toward the enemies of our land, the disturbers of public peace, and the menacers of the social conventions of our time and land. The public welfare requires that we inhibit our fighting impulses, except in cases of self-defense or war. Public policy requires that we keep our ambitions within reasonable limits, which limits change from time to time, of course. In short, society has stepped in and insisted that man, as a social being, must not only acquire a *social conscience* but must also develop sociable emotions and inhibit his unsociable ones. The evolution of man's nature has caused him unconsciously to modify his elemental, instinctive, passional emotions, and subordinate them to the dictates of social, ethical, moral, and æsthetic feelings and ideals, and to intellectual considerations. Even the original elemental instincts of the lower animals have been modified by reason of the social requirements of the pack, herd, or drove, until the modified instinct is now the ruling force.

The general principles of emotional control, restraint, and mastery, as given in a preceding chapter, are applicable to the particular class of emotions now under consideration here.

(1) By refraining from the physical expression, one may at least partially inhibit the emotion.

(2) By refusing to create the habit, one may more easily manifest control.

(3) By refusing to dwell upon the idea or mental picture of the exciting object, one may lessen the stimulus.

(4) By cultivating the opposite class of emotions, one may inhibit any class of feeling.

(5) And, finally, by acquiring a control of the attention, by means of the will, one has the reins firmly in hand, and may drive or hold back the steeds of passion as he wills.

The passions are like fiery horses, useful if well under control, but most dangerous if the control is lost. The ego is the driver, the will his hands, attention the reins, habit the bit, and the passions the horses. To drive the chariot of life under social conditions, the ego must have strong hands (will) to tighten or loosen the reins of attention. He must also employ a well designed and shaped bit of habit. Without strong hands, good reins, and well-adjusted bit, the fiery steeds of passion may gain control and, running away, dash the chariot and its driver over the precipice and on to the jagged rocks below.

14
The Social Emotions

AS man became a social animal he developed new traits of character, new habits of action, new ideals, new customs, and consequently new emotions. Emotions long entertained and long manifested by the race become more or less instinctive, and are passed along in the form of either (*a*) inherited stimulus akin to, but lesser in degree and force than, the more elemental emotions; or (*b*) of inherited *tendency* to manifest the acquired emotional feeling upon the presentation of sufficiently strong stimuli. Hence arises that which we have called "the social emotions."

Under the classification of "the social emotions" are those acquired tendencies of action and feeling of the race which are more or less altruistic, and are concerned with the welfare of others and one's duties and obligations toward society and our fellow men. In this class are found the emotions which impel us to perform what we consider or feel to be our duty toward our neighbors, and our obligations and duty toward the state, as expressed in its laws, the customs of men of our country, or the ideals of the community. In another phase it manifests as sympathy, fellow feeling, and "kindness" in general. In its first phase we find civic virtue, law-abiding inclination, honesty, "square dealing," and patriotism; in its second phase we find sympathy for others, charity, mutual aid, the alleviation of poverty and suffering, the erection of asylums for orphans and the aged, hospitals for the sick, and the formation of societies for general charitable work.

In many cases we find the social, ethical, and moral emotions closely allied with religious emotion, and by many these are supposed to be practically identical, but there is a vast difference in spite of their frequent association. For instance, we find many persons of high civic virtue, of exalted moral ideals, and manifesting ethical qualities of the most advanced type, who are lacking in the ordinary religious feelings. On the other hand, we too frequently find persons professing great religious zeal, and apparently experiencing the most intense religious emotional feeling, who are deficient in social, civic, ethical, and moral qualities, in the best sense of these terms. The aim of all religion worthy of the name, however, is to encourage ethical and moral as well as religious emotions.

We must here make the distinction between those manifesting the actions termed ethical and moral *because they feel that way*, and those who merely comply with the conventional requirements *because they fear the consequences* of their violation. The first class have the true social, ethical, and moral feelings, tastes, ideals, and inclinations; while the second manifest merely the elementary feelings of self-preservation and selfish prudence. The first class are "good" because they feel that way and find it natural to be so; while the others are "good" merely because they have to be or be punished by legal penalty or public opinion, loss of prestige, loss of financial support, etc.

The social, moral, and ethical emotions are believed to have arisen in the race by reason of the association of individuals in communities and the rise of the necessity for mutual aid and forbearance. Even many of the species of the lower animals have social, moral, or ethical codes of their own, based on the experience of the species or family, infractions of which they punish severely. In the same way sympathy and the altruistic feelings are supposed to have arisen. The community of interest and understanding in the tribe, family, or clan brought not only the feeling of natural defense and protection but also the finer, inner sympathetic feeling of the pains and sufferings of their associates. This, in the progress of the race, has developed into broader and more complex ideals and feelings.

Theology explains the moral feelings as resulting from conscience, which it holds to be a special faculty of the mind, or soul, divinely given. Science, while admitting the existence of the state of feelings which we call "conscience," denies its supernatural origin, and ascribes it to the result of evolution, heredity, experience, education, and suggestion. Conscience, according to science, is a compound of intellectual and emotional states. Conscience is not an invariable or infallible guide, but *depends entirely upon the heredity, education, experience, and environment of the individual.* It accompanies the moral and ethical codes of the race, which vary with time and with country. Actions which were thought right a century ago are condemned now; likewise, things condemned a century ago are thought right now. What is commended in Turkey is condemned in England, and vice versa. Moral tastes and ideals, like æsthetic ones, vary with time and country. There is no absolute code which has been always true, in all places. There is an evolution in the ideals of morals and ethics as in everything else, and "conscience" and the moral and ethical emotions accompany the changing ideals.

Many of the moral and ethical principles originally arose from necessity or utility, but have since developed into natural, spontaneous feeling on the part of the race. It is held that the race is rapidly developing a "social conscience" which will cause the wiping out of many social conditions which are now the disgrace of civilization. It is predicted that in time the race will look back upon the existence of poverty in our civilization as our generation now looks back upon the existence of slavery, imprisonment for debt, capital punishment for the theft of a loaf of bread, the killing of prisoners of war, etc. It is thought that, in time, wars of conquest will be deemed as utterly immoral as to-day is regarded the murder of a body of men by a band of pirates or bandits. In the same way the economic slavery of to-day will be seen as immoral as now seems the physical slavery of the past. In not far distant time it will seem incredible that society could have ever allowed one of its members to die of hunger in the streets, or of poverty and inattention in the sick room of the hovel. Not only will the ideals and feelings of ethical and moral responsibility change and evolve, but the feelings of personal sympathy will evolve in accordance therewith. At least such is the dream and prophecy of some of the world's greatest thinkers.

The social, ethical, and moral emotions may be developed by a study of the evolution and meaning of society on the one hand, and the perception of the condition of the lives of less fortunate individuals on the other. The first will awaken new ideas of the history and real meaning of social association and mutual intercourse, and will develop a new sense of responsibility, duty, and civic and social pride. The second will awaken understanding and sympathy, and a desire to do what one can to help those who are "the under dog," and also to bring about a better state of affairs in general. The study of history and civilization, of sociology and civics, will do much in the first direction. The study of human-kind, and its life problems and condition, will do the same in the second case. In both cases there will be awakened a new sense of "right and wrong"—a new conception of "ought and ought not"—regarding one's relations to the race, society, and his fellow beings.

Let no one deceive himself or herself by the smug assumption that the race has entirely emerged from barbarism and is now on the top wave of civilization. The truth, as known to all careful and conscientious thinkers, is that we are but *half* civilized, if, indeed, that much. Many of our customs and conventions are those of a half-barbarous people. Our ideals are low, our customs often vile. We lack not only high ideals but in many cases we show a lack of sanity in our social conventions. But evolution is moving us slowly ahead. A better day is dawning. The signs are in the air, to be seen by all thoughtful men. Civilization is climbing the ladder, aided by the evolution of the social, ethical, and moral emotions and the development of the intellect.

In connection with this phase of the emotions, we invite the student to consider the following excellent words of Professor Davidson in his "History of Greek Education":

"It is not enough for a man to understand the conditions of rational life in his own time. He must likewise *love* these conditions and *hate* whatever leads to life of an opposite kind. This is only another way of saying that he must love the good and hate the evil; for the good is simply what conduces to rational or moral life, and the evil simply what leads away from it. It is perfectly obvious, as soon as it is pointed out, that all immoral life is due to a false distribution of affection, which again is often, though by no means always, due to a want of intellectual cultivation. He that attributes to anything a value greater or less than it really possesses, in the order of things, has already placed himself in a false relation to it, and will certainly, when he comes to act with reference to it, act immorally."

15
The Religious Emotions

BY "the religious emotions" is meant that class of emotional feeling arising from the faith and belief in, or consciousness of the presence of, supernatural beings, powers, entities, or forces. This form of emotion is regarded as distinct from the ethical and moral emotions, although frequently found in connection therewith. Likewise, it is independent of any special form of intellectual belief, for it is far more fundamental and often exists without creed, philosophy, or stated belief, the only manifestation in such cases being a "feeling" of the existence of supernatural beings, forces, and powers to which man has a relation and to which he owes obedience. To those who may think that this is too narrow a conception of religious emotion we refer the following definition of "religion" from the dictionaries: "The acts or feelings which result from the belief of a god, or gods, having superior control over matter, life, or destiny. Religion is subjective, designating the feelings and acts of men which relate to God; theology is objective, denoting the science which investigates the existence, laws, and attributes of God;" or (objectively) "the outer form and embodiment which the inward spirit of a true or a false devotion assumes," (subjectively) "the feeling of veneration with which the worshiper regards the Being he adores."

Darwin, in his "Descent of Man," says that the feeling of religious devotion is a highly complex one, consisting of love, complete submission to an exalted and mysterious superior, a strong sense of dependence, fear, reverence, gratitude, hope for the future, and perhaps other elements. He is of the opinion that no man can experience so complex an emotion until advanced in his intellectual and moral faculties to at least a moderately high level. The authorities generally agree with Darwin, although the more recent study of the history of religion has shown that religious feeling has a far more primitive origin than that indicated by Darwin.

It is true that the lower animals are not deemed capable of anything approaching religious feeling, unless there is a feeling approaching it in the attitude of the dog and horse and other domestic animals toward their masters. But man, as soon as he is able to attribute natural phenomena to a supernatural cause and power, manifests a crude religious feeling and emotion. He begins by believing in, fearing, and worshiping natural forces and objects, such as the sun, the moon, the wind, thunder and lightning, the ocean, rivers, mountains, etc. It is claimed that there is no natural object that has not been deified and worshiped by some people at some time in the history of the race. Later, man acquired the anthropomorphic conception of deities and created many gods in his own image, endowing them with his own attributes, qualities, and characteristics. The mental characteristics and morals of a people can always be ascertained by a knowledge of the average conception of deity held by them. Polytheism, or the belief in many gods, was succeeded by monotheism, or belief in one god.

Monotheism ranges from the crudest conception of a manlike god to the highest conception of a spiritual Being transcending all human qualities, attributes, or characteristics. Man began by believing in many god *things*, then in many god *persons*, then in a one god-person, then in one God who is a spirit, then in One Universal Spirit which is God. It is a far cry from the savage, manlike god of old to the conception of the Universal Spirit of the "God-drunken philosopher," Spinoza. The extreme of religious belief is that which holds that "there is nothing but God—all else is illusion," of pantheistic idealism. Buddhism (at least in its original form) discarded the idea of a Supreme Being, and held that Ultimate Reality is but Universal *Law*; hence the accusation that Buddhism is an "atheistic religion," although it is one of the world's greatest religions, having over 400,000,000 followers.

But the *beliefs* of the religious person may be considered as resulting from intellectual processes; his religious *feelings and emotions* arise from another part of his mental being. It is the testimony of the authorities of all religions that religious conviction is an inner experience rather than an intellectual conception. The emotional element is always active in religious manifestations everywhere. The purely intellectual religion is naught but a philosophy. Religion without feeling and emotion is an anomaly. In all true religion there exists a feeling of inner assurance and faith, love, awe, dependence, submission, reverence, gratitude, hope, and perhaps fear. The emotional element must always be present, not necessarily in the form of emotional excess, as in the case of revival hysteria or the dance of the whirling dervishes, but at least in the form of the calm, fervent feeling of "that peace which passeth understanding." When religion departs from the emotional phase it becomes merely a "school of philosophy," or an "ethical culture society."

The student must not lose sight of the uplifting influence of true religious emotion by reason of his knowledge of its lowly origin. Like the lotus, which has its roots in the slimy, filthy mud of the river, and its stem in the muddy, stagnant, and foul waters thereof, but its beautiful flower unfolded in the clear air and facing the sun, so is religious feeling responsible for some of the most beautiful and uplifting ideals and actions of the race. If its origin and history contain much that is not consistent with the highest ideals of the race to-day, it is not the fault of religion but of the race itself. Religion, like all else in the universal manifestation, is under the laws of evolution, growth, and development. What the religion of the future may be, we know not. But the prophets of the race are dreaming visions of a religion as much higher than that of to-day as the latter is higher than the crude fetichism of the savage.

The following quotation from John Fiske's "Through Nature to God" is appropriate in this place. Fiske says: "My aim is to show that 'that other influence,' that inward conviction, the craving for a final cause, the theistic assumption, is itself one of the master facts of the universe, and as much entitled to respect as any fact in physical nature can possibly be. The argument flashed upon me about ten years ago while reading Herbert Spencer's controversy with Frederic Harrison concerning the nature and reality of religion. Because Spencer derived historically the greater part of modern belief in an Unseen World from the savage's primeval world of dreams and ghosts, some of his critics maintained that logical consistency required him to dismiss the modern belief as utterly false; otherwise he would be guilty of seeking to evolve truth from falsehood. 'By no means,' replied Spencer. 'Contrariwise, the ultimate form of the religious consciousness is the final development of a consciousness which at the outset contained a germ of truth obscured by multitudinous errors.'" Fiske, in this connection, quotes the Tennysonian question:—

"'Who forged that other influence,
That heat of inward evidence,
By which he doubts against the sense?'"

The religious emotions may be developed by allowing the mind to dwell upon the Power underlying the universe of fleeting, changing forms; by reading prose and poetry in which an appeal is made to the religious instinct; by listening to music which awakens the emotion of reverence and awe; and, finally, by meditating upon the inner spirit immanent in every living being. As an old Hindu sage once said: "There are many paths by which men arrive at a knowledge of the presence of God, but there is but one goal and destination."

16
The Aesthetic Emotions

BY "the æsthetic emotions" is meant those emotional feelings which are concerned with the perception of beauty or taste, and by reason of which we "like" or "dislike" certain perceptions of sensory impressions. In order to get a clearer idea, let us consider what is meant by "beauty" and "taste."

"Beauty" is defined as "that quality or assemblage of qualities in an object which gives the eye or the ear intense pleasure; or that characteristic in an object which gratifies the intellect or moral feeling." "Taste" (in this sense of the term) is defined as "nice perception, or the power of perceiving and relishing excellence in human performances; the power of appreciating the finer qualities of art; the faculty of discerning beauty, order, congruity, proportion, symmetry, or whatever constitutes excellence, particularly in the fine arts or literature; the faculty of the mind by which we both perceive and enjoy whatever is beautiful or sublime in the works of nature and art. The possession of taste insures grace and beauty in the works of an artist, and the avoidance of all that is low or mean. It is as often the result of an innate sense of beauty or propriety as of art education, and no genius can compensate for the want of it.

* * *

Tastes differ so much among individuals, nations, or in different ages and conditions of civilization that it is utterly impossible to set up a standard of taste applicable to all men and to all stages in the evolution of society."

The æsthetic sense, feeling, and emotion are products of the later stages of the evolution of the mind of man. Their roots, however, may be seen in the crude attempts at decoration and adornment in the savage, and still further back in the tendency of certain birds to adorn their nests or "bowers." Moreover, some sense of beauty must exist in the lower animals, which are influenced thereby in the selection of their mates, the bright plumage of the birds, and the coloring of the insects and higher animals evidencing the existence of at least a primitive æsthetic sense. Herbert Spencer says that one characteristic of the æsthetic feelings is that they are separated from the functions vitally requisite and necessary to sustain life, and it is not until the latter are reasonably well satisfied that the former begin to manifest in force.

The authorities hold that the basic element concerned in the manifestation of the æsthetic emotional feeling is the *sensory* element, which consists of the pleasure arising from the perception of objects of vision or hearing which are deemed beautiful. There is a certain nervous satisfaction which arises from the perception of the sensation of the sight of a beautiful thing, or of the hearing of beautiful sound. Just *why* certain sights prove agreeable and others disagreeable, or certain sounds pleasant and others unpleasant, is very difficult to determine. Association and habit may have something to do with the beauty of sight object, and there may be natural harmony of vibration in colors as there is in sound. In the case of sounds there is undoubtedly a natural harmony between the vibrations of certain notes of the scale and inharmony between others. Some have held that the secret of the enjoyment of music is found in the natural appreciation of rhythm, as rhythm is a cosmic manifestation evident in everything from great to small. But these theories do not account for the differences existing in the tastes regarding color and music manifested by different individuals, races, and classes of people.

Grant Allen says: "The vulgar are pleased with great masses of color, especially red, orange, and purple, which give their coarse, nervous organization the requisite stimulus. The refined, with nerves of less caliber, but greater discriminativeness, require delicate combinations of complementaries and prefer neutral tints to the glare of the primary hues. Children and savages love to dress in all the colors of the rainbow." In the same way persons of certain types of taste are pleased with "rag time" and cheap, rollicking songs or dances, while others shudder at these and find delight in the classic productions of the great composers.

There is also the *intellectual* element to be reckoned with in the æsthetic emotions. The intellect must discover the beauty in certain objects before the emotion is aroused by the perception. Halleck says: "Every time the mind discerns unity amid variety, order, rhythm, proportion, or symmetry, an æsthetic emotion arises.

* * *

The traveler with a trained intellect will see far more beauty than an ignorant one. In looking at a cathedral, a large part of the æsthetic enjoyment comes from tracing out the symmetry, from comparing part with part. Not until this process is complete will the full beauty of the structure as a whole be perceived. If the traveler knows something of mediæval architecture before starting on his European trip, he will see far more beauty. The opposite of the æsthetic, which we call the ugly, is the unsymmetrical, the disorderly—that in which we can discover no rhythm, plan, or beauty."

The element of *associative suggestion* also enters into the manifestation of æsthetic emotional feeling. The mind accepts the suggestion of the beauty of certain styles of art, or the excellence of certain classes of music. There are fashions in art and music, as in clothes, and what is thought beautiful to-day may be deemed hideous to-morrow. This is not entirely due to the evolution of taste, for in many cases the old fashions are revived and again deemed beautiful. There is, moreover, the effect of the association of the object of emotion with certain events or persons. This association renders the thing popular, and therefore agreeable and beautiful for the time being. The suggestion in a story will often cause the beauty of a certain scene, or the harmony of a certain piece of music, to dawn upon thousands of persons. Some noted person sets the seal of approval upon a certain picture or musical composition and lo! the multitude calls it beautiful. It must not be supposed, however, that the crowd always counterfeits this sense of beauty and excellence which has been suggested to it. On the contrary, genuine æsthetic feeling often results from the discovery so made.

There is style and fashion in the use of words, resulting from fashion, which gives rise to æsthetic feelings regarding them. These feelings do not arise from the consideration of the nature of the object expressed by the word; of two words designating the same thing, one causes disgust and the other at least passive tolerance. For instance, in speaking of the sensible moisture which is emitted from the pores of the skin, we may use either of the respective terms "sweat" or "perspiration." Both mean the same thing, and have an equally respectable origin. But to many persons the word "sweat" causes unpleasant æsthetic emotion, while the word "perspiration" is accepted without remonstrance. Some persons abhor the term "victuals," while "viands" or "food" are accepted without protest. There is often an unpleasant, low, vulgar association connected with some words which accounts for the disfavor with which they are received, and which association is absent from the more "polite" terms employed to indicate the same thing. But in other cases there is nothing but the simple suggestion of fashion and style to account for the æsthetic acceptance or rejection.

It is possible that some psychologist of the future will establish the truth of the theory now tentatively advanced by a few investigators, namely, that taste and the sense of beauty depend almost entirely upon the element of suggestion, manifested as association, influence of authority, habit, fashion, imitation, etc. It is known that the emotional nature is peculiarly liable to suggestion, and that tastes may be created or destroyed by repeated suggestion under the most favorable circumstances. It is thought likely that if we could trace back to its roots every emotion of taste, we would find it arising from some associative, suggestive influence connected with another and more elemental class of emotions.

Regarding the fact that there is no universal standard of taste or beauty, Halleck says: "It has been said that æsthetics cannot be treated in a scientific way because there is no standard of taste. '*De gustibus non est disputandum*' ('there is no disputing about tastes') is an old proverb. Of two equally intelligent persons, the one may like a certain book, the other dislike it.

* * *

While it is true that the standard of taste is a varying one within certain limits, it is no more so than that of morals. As men's nervous systems, education, and associations differ, we may scientifically conclude that their tastes must differ. The greater the uniformity in the factors the less does the product vary. On the other hand, within certain limits, the standard of æsthetics is relatively uniform. *It is fixed by the majority of intelligent people of any age and country.* To estimate the standard by which to judge of the correctness of language or of the literary taste of any era, we examine the conversations of the best speakers, the works of the standard writers."

The æsthetic emotions may be developed and cultivated by exercise and practice, and particularly by association and familiarity with beautiful things, and with those who have "good taste." Appreciation of beauty is more or less contagious, up to a certain point of development, at least, and if one wishes to recognize, understand, and appreciate beauty, he should go where beauty is, and where its votaries are gathered. The study of standard works of art, or objects of nature, or the best productions of the composers of music, will do much to develop and unfold one's higher æsthetic feelings and understanding.

It is claimed by some of the best authorities that to develop the finer and higher æsthetic feelings and understanding we must learn to find beauty and excellence in things removed from ourselves or our selfish interests. The narrow, selfish emotions kill the æsthetic feelings—the two cannot exist together. The person whose thoughts are centered on himself or herself very rarely finds beauty or excellence in works of art or music. Grant Allen well sums up the subject in the following words: "*Good taste is the progressive product of progressing fineness and discrimination in the nerves, educated attention, high and noble emotional constitution, and increasing intellectual faculties.*"

17
The Intellectual Emotions

BY "the intellectual emotions" is meant that class of emotional feeling resulting from the presence of objects of intellectual interest. This class of emotions depends for its satisfaction upon the exercise of the intellectual faculties, from the most simple to the most complex, and including perception, memory, imagination, reason, judgment, and all the logical faculties. Those who are accustomed to employing the mind through voluntary attention, particularly in the direction of creative ideation or constructive imagination, experience these emotions to a greater or less degree.

The exercise of perception, if we are skilled therein, gives us a pleasurable feeling, and if we succeed in making an interesting or important discovery by reason thereof, we experience a strong degree of emotional satisfaction. Likewise, we experience agreeable feelings when we are able to remember distinctly something which might well have been forgotten, or when we succeed in recalling something which had escaped our memory for the moment. In the same way the exercise of the imagination is a source of great pleasure in many cases in the direction of writing, planning, inventing, or other creative processes, or even in the building of air castles. The exercise of the logical faculties gives great pleasure to those in whom these faculties are well developed.

Halleck well says: "There was probably not a happier moment in Newton's life than when he had succeeded in demonstrating that the same power which caused the apple to fall held the moon and the planets in their orbits. When Watts discovered that steam might be harnessed like a horse, when an inventor succeeds in perfecting a labor-lightening device, whenever an obscurity is cleared away, the reason for a thing understood, and a baffling instance brought under a general law, intellectual emotion results."

The pleasurable feelings we experience upon the reading of a good book, or the discovery of real poetry, are forms of intellectual emotion. The same class of emotional feeling is aroused when we witness a good play. Among other instances of this class we mention the perception of clever work of any kind, intricate machinery, ingenious devices, helpful improvements, or other works of man which indicate the existence of thought and inventive ability in the designer or builder. To appreciate mental work of this kind we must bring a mind developed along the same or similar lines. It has well been said that before one can take away anything from a book he must bring something to it. It takes mentality to recognize and appreciate mentality or the work of mentality.

The study of scientific subjects is a source of great pleasure to those who are inclined to such pursuits. To the scientific mind the study of the latest work on the favorite branch gives a joy which nothing else is capable of arousing. To the philosopher the works of other philosophers of the same school give intense satisfaction.

It is claimed that the sense of humor and wit is an intellectual emotion, for it depends upon the detection of the ludicrous features of a happening. Certain psychologists have held that the distinctive element of humor is the feeling attendant upon the perception of incongruity; while that of wit is the feeling of superiority on the part of the witty person, and the corresponding chagrin of the object of his wit. It would seem, however, that the appreciation of wit must depend upon the intellectual perception of cleverness of expression and the pleasure resulting from the discovery thereof, and that the feeling of humor is aroused principally by reason of the incongruous element; the feeling of self-satisfaction as contrasted with the discomfiture of the other person belongs to the more selfish emotions. An authority says: "Humor is a mental faculty which tends to discover incongruous resemblances between things which essentially differ, or essential differences between things put forth as the same, the result being internal mirth or an outburst of laughter. Wit does so likewise, but the two are different. Humor has deep human sympathy, and loves men while raising a laugh against their weaknesses. Wit is deficient in sympathy, and there is often a sting in its ridicule. Somewhat contemptuous of mankind, it has not the patience to study them thoroughly, but must content itself with noting superficial resemblances or differences. Humor is patient and keenly observant, and penetrates beneath the surface; while, therefore, the sallies of wit are often one-sided and unfair, those of humor are, as a rule, just and wise."

The development and cultivation of the intellectual emotions depend, of course, upon education, training, exercise, and practice. The cultivation of the intellect (which has been referred to, in part, in the previous parts of this book, and which will be again considered in the chapters devoted to the intellect) results in the development and cultivation of the emotions accompanying intellectual effort. In a general way, however, it may be said that the reading of the best works of fiction, science, and philosophy will bring out in time the best form of intellectual enjoyment and feeling. The highest gives the best—that is the rule. The present chapter should be read and studied in connection with those devoted to the intellect.

Blended Emotions

As we have said at the beginning of our consideration of the subject of the emotions, the majority of emotions are composed of several feelings, and tend to blend and combine emotional elements. For instance, the emotion of sexual love certainly has its origin in the instinctive feelings of the race, and its motive element is that of passion. But passion is far from being all there is in human sexual love. Above the plane of passion is found the social emotion of companionship, protection, and care; the desire for the welfare of the loved one; the mingling of the love of the parent with that of the mate. Human love manifests many of the altruistic emotions during its course. The welfare of the loved one becomes the chief concern of life, often stronger even than self-preservation. The joy of the loved one becomes the greatest joy, far surpassing the more selfish forms of happiness. Then come the æsthetic feelings, which find satisfaction in the two "liking the same things," sympathy and community of feeling being the connecting link. The several ideals of the two combining, there is produced an idealistic union, which is often called "spiritual harmony." Finally, there is found the blending of the intellectual emotions, in which harmony there exists one of the highest forms of pleasure satisfaction between two persons of opposite sexes. It is said that the more things that a man and woman "like" in common, the closer will be their "liking" for each other. "I love you because you love the things I love," is no rare thought and expression.

So it is seen that though born in elemental instinct and passion, human sexual love is something far different in its flowering. And yet without its root it would not be, and cannot be. This is an excellent example of the complex nature of the most common emotions. It may be used as a typical illustration. What is true of it is also true, in a way and in a degree, of every other form of emotion. Therefore in studying a particular emotion, be not too quick to cry, "It is this; it is that!" but rather seek to say, "It is composed of this and that, of this and that!" Few, if any, emotions are simple; the majority are very complex. Hence the difficulty of satisfactory classification, and the danger of dogmatic definition.

18

The Role Of The Emotions

THE average person greatly underestimates the part played by the emotional nature in the mental activities of the individual. He is inclined to the opinion that, with the exception of the occasional manifestation of some strong emotional feeling, the majority of persons go through life using only the reasoning and reflective faculties in deciding the problems of life and guiding the mental course of action. There can be no greater mistake concerning the mental activities. So far from being subordinate to the intellect, the emotional nature in the majority of cases dominates the reasoning faculties. There are but very few persons who are able to detach themselves, even in a small degree, from the feelings, and to decide questions cold-bloodedly by pure reason or intellectual effort. Moreover, there are but few persons whose wills are guided by pure reason; the feelings supply the motive for the majority of acts of will. The intellect, even when used, is generally employed to better carry out the dictates of feeling and desire. Much of our reasoning is performed in order to justify our feelings, or to find proofs for the position dictated by our desires, feelings, sympathies, prejudices, or sentiments. It has been said that "men seek not reasons but *excuses for their actions*."

Moreover, in the elementary processes of the intellect the emotions play an important part. We have seen that attention largely follows interest, and interest results from feeling. Therefore our attention, and that which arises from it, is dependent largely upon the feelings. Thus feeling asserts its power in guarding the very outer gate of knowledge, and determines largely what shall or shall not enter therein. It is one of the constantly-appearing paradoxes of psychology, that while feelings have originally arisen from attention, it is equally true that attention depends largely upon the interest resulting from the feelings. This is readily admitted in the case of involuntary attention, which always goes out toward objects of interest and feeling, but is likewise true of even voluntary attention, which we direct to something of greater or more nearly ultimate interest than the things of lesser or more immediate interest.

Sully says: "By an act of will I may resolve to turn my attention to something—say a passage in a book. But if, after the preliminary process of adjustment of the mental eye the object opens up no interesting phase, all the willing in the world will not produce a calm, settled state of concentration. The will introduces mind and object; it cannot force an attachment between them. No compulsion of attention ever succeeded in making a young child cordially embrace and appropriate, by an act of concentration, an unsuitable and therefore uninteresting object. We thus see that even voluntary interest is not removed from the sway of interest. What the will *does* is to determine *the kind of interest* that shall prevail at the moment."

Again, we may see that memory is largely dependent upon interest in recording and recalling its impressions. We remember and recall most easily that which most greatly interests us. In proportion to the lack of interest in a thing do we find difficulty in remembering or recalling it. This is equally true of the imagination, for it refuses to dwell upon that which is *not* interesting. Even in the reasoning processes we find the will balking at uninteresting subjects, but galloping along, pushing before it the rolling chair of interesting intellectual application.

Our judgments are affected by our feelings. It is much easier to approve of the actions of some person we like, or whose views accord with our own, than of an individual whose personality and views are distasteful to us. It is very difficult to prevent prejudice, for or against, from influencing our judgments. It is also true that we "find that for which we look" in things and persons, and that which we expect and look for is often dependent upon our feelings. If we dislike a person or thing we are usually able to perceive no end of undesirable things in him or it; while if we are favorably inclined we easily find many admirable qualities in the same person or thing. A little change in our feeling often results in the formation of an entirely new set of judgments regarding a person or thing.

Halleck well says: "On the one hand the emotions are favorable to intellectual action, since they supply the interest one feels in study. One may feel intensely concerning a certain subject and be all the better student. Hence the emotions are not, as was formerly thought, entirely hostile to intellectual action. Emotion often quickens the perception, burns things indelibly into the memory, and doubles the rapidity of thought. On the other hand strong feelings often vitiate every operation of the intellect. They cause us to see only what we wish to, to remember only what interests our narrow feeling at the time, and to reason from selfish data only.

* * *

Emotion puts the magnifying end of the telescope to our intellectual eyes where our own interests are concerned, the minimizing end when we are looking at the interest of others.

* * *

Thought is deflected when it passes through an emotional medium, just as a sunbeam is when it strikes water."

As for the will, the best authorities hold that it is almost if not entirely dependent upon desire for its motive force. As desire is an outgrowth and development of feeling and emotion, it is seen that even the will depends upon feeling for its inciting motives and its direction. We shall consider this point at greater detail in the chapters devoted to the activities of the will.

We would remind you again, at this point, of the great triangle of the mind, the emotional, ideative, and volitional activities—feeling, thinking, and willing—and their constant reaction upon each other and absolute interdependence. We find that our feelings arise from previous willing and ideation, and are aroused by ideas and repressed by will; again we see that our ideas are largely dependent upon the interest supplied by our feelings, and that our judgments are influenced by the emotive side of our mental life, the will also having its part to play in the matter. We also see that the will is called into activity by the feelings, and often guided or restrained by our thoughts, the will, indeed, being considered as moved entirely by our feelings and ideas. Thus is the trinity of mental forces seen ever in mutual relation—constant action and reaction ever existing between them.

19

The Emotions And Happiness

"HAPPINESS" has been defined by an authority as "the pleasurable emotion arising from the gratification of all desires; the enjoyment of pleasure without pain." Another has said that "happiness is the state in which all desires are satisfied." But these definitions have been attacked. It is held by many that a state of the absolute *satisfaction* of desire would not be happiness, for happiness consists largely in pleasurable anticipation and imaginings which disappear upon the realization of the desire. It is held that absolute satisfaction would be a negative state. Paley expressed a better idea when he said that "any condition may be denominated 'happy' in which the amount or aggregate of pleasure exceeds that of pain, and the degree of happiness depends upon the quantity of this excess."

Some have held that an existing contrast between pain and pleasure (the balance being in favor of the latter) is necessary to establish happiness. Be this as it may, it is admitted by all that one's happiness or unhappiness depends entirely upon one's emotional nature and the degree of the satisfaction thereof. And it is generally admitted that to be happy is the great aim and object of the life of the majority of persons,—if, indeed, not of *every* person,—the happiness, of course, depending upon the quality and degree of the emotions forming the person's emotional nature. Thus it is seen that we are dependent upon the emotional side of our mental life in this as in nearly everything else making life worth while.

Theologians have often sought to point out that happiness is not the goal of life and living, but human nature has always insisted that happiness is the greatest end, and philosophy has generally supported it. But wisdom shows that happiness is not always dependent upon the pleasure of the moment, for the sacrifice of immediate pleasure frequently results in a much greater happiness in the future. In the same way an immediate disagreeable task often gains for us a greater satisfaction in the future. Likewise, it is frequently greater happiness to sacrifice a personal pleasure for the happiness of others than it would be to enjoy the pleasure of the moment at the expense of the pain of the other. There is often a far greater pleasure resulting from an altruistic action of self-sacrifice than in the performance of the selfish, egoistic act. But, as the subtle reasoner may insist, the result is the same—the ultimate happiness and satisfaction of the self. This conclusion does not rob the altruistic act of its virtue, however, for the person who finds his greatest pleasure in giving pleasure to others is to be congratulated—as is the community which shelters him.

There is no virtue in pain, suffering, sacrifice, or unhappiness *for its own sake*. This illusion of asceticism is vanishing from the human mind. Sacrifice on the part of the individual is valuable and valid only when it results in higher present or future happiness for the individual or some one else. There is no virtue in pain, physical or mental, except as a step to a greater good for ourselves or others. Pain at the best is merely nature's alarm and warning of "not this way." It is also held that pain serves to bring out pleasure by contrast, and is therefore valuable in this way. Be this as it may, no normal individual deliberately seeks ultimate pain in preference to ultimate happiness; the greatest ultimate happiness to one's self and to those he loves is the normal and natural goal of the normal person. But the concept of "those he loves," in many cases, includes the race as well as the immediate family.

Wisdom shows the individual that the greatest happiness comes to him who controls and restrains many of his feelings. Dissipation results in pain and unhappiness ultimately. The doctrine of thoughtless indulgence is unphilosophical and is contradicted by the experience of the race. Moreover, wisdom shows that the highest happiness comes not from the indulgence of the physical feelings alone, or to excess, but rather from the cultivation, development, and manifestation of the higher feelings—the social, æsthetic, and intellectual emotions. The higher pleasures of life, literature, art, music, science, invention, constructive imagination, etc., yield a satisfaction and happiness keener and more enduring than can possibly the lower forms of feeling. But the human being must not despise any part of his emotional being. Everything has its uses, which are good; and its abuses, which are bad. Every part of one's being, mental and physical, is well to use; but no part is well used if it uses the individual instead of being itself used.

A recent writer has held that the end and aim of life should not be the pursuit of happiness, but rather the building of character. The obvious answer is that the two are identical in spirit, for to the man who appreciates the value of character, its attainment is the greatest happiness; the wise teach that the greatest happiness comes to him who is possessed of a well-rounded, developed character. Another writer has said that "the aim of life should be self-improvement, with a due regard to the interest of others." This is but saying that the greatest happiness to the wise man lies in this course. Any one who is wise enough, or great enough, to make these ends the aim and goal of life will find the greatest happiness therefrom. Arnold Bennett advances as a good working philosophy of life: "cheerfulness, kindliness, and rectitude." Can any one doubt that this course would bring great ultimate happiness?

Happiness consists in that which "contents the spirit," and the latter depends entirely upon the character of the feelings and emotions entertained by one, as weighed in the balance of reason, and as passed upon by judgment and the sense of right action. The greatest degree of happiness, or at least the greatest ratio of pleasure over pain, is obtained by a careful and intelligent cultivation of the feeling side of one's being in connection with the cultivation of the intellect and the mastery of the will. To be able to bring the capacity for enjoyment to its highest; to be able to intelligently choose that which will bring the greatest ultimate happiness in accordance with right action; and, finally, to be able to use the will in the direction of holding fast to that which is good and rejecting that which is bad—this is the power of creating happiness. The feelings, the intellect, and the will—here, as ever—combine to manifest the result.

Finally, it must be remembered that all human happiness consists in part of the ability to bear pain—to suffer. There must be the dash of Stoicism in the wise Epicurean. One must learn to pluck from pain, suffering, and unhappiness the secret drop of honey which lies at its heart, and which consists in the knowledge of the meaning and use of pain and the means whereby it may be transmuted into knowledge and experience, from which later happiness may be distilled. To profit by pain, to transmute suffering into joy, to transform present unhappiness into a future greater happiness—this is the privilege of the philosopher.

The mental states and activities known as "desire" are a direct development of the feeling and emotional phase of the mind and form the motive power of the will. Desire, in fact, may be said to be composed of feeling on one side and will on the other. But the influence of the intellect or reasoning faculties has a most important part to play in the evolution of feeling into desire, and in the consequent action of the will by the presentation and weighing of conflicting desires. Therefore, the logical place for the consideration of the activities of the intellect is at this point—between emotion and will. Accordingly, we shall leave the subject of feeling and emotion for the present, to be taken up again in connection with the subject of *desire*, after we have considered the intellectual processes of the mind. But, as has been indicated, we shall see the presence and influence of the feelings and emotions even in the activities of the intellect.

20
The Intellect

THE class of mental states or processes grouped together under the name of "intellectual processes," forms the second great division of the mental states, the two others being "feeling" and "will," respectively.

"Intellect" has been defined as follows: "The part or faculty of the human mind by which it knows, as distinguished from the power to feel and to will; the thinking faculty; the understanding;" also as "that faculty of the human mind by which it receives or comprehends the ideas communicated to it by the senses or the perception, or other means, as distinguished from the power to feel and to will; the power or faculty to perceive objects in their relations; the power to judge and comprehend; also the capacity for higher forms of knowledge, as distinguished from the power to perceive and imagine."

In the preceding chapters we have seen that the individual is able to experience sensations in consciousness, and that he is able to *perceive* them mentally, the latter being the first step in intellectual activity. We have also seen that he is able to reproduce the perception by means of memory and imagination, and that by means of the latter he is able to re-combine and rearrange the objects of perception. We have also seen that he has what are known as "feelings," which depend upon his previous experience and that of his progenitors. So far the mind has been considered merely as a receiving and reproducing instrument, with the added attachment of the re-combining power of the imagination. Up to this point the mind may be compared to the phonographic cylinder, with an attachment capable of re-combining its recorded impressions. The impressions are received and perceived, are stored away, are reproduced, and by the use of the imagination are re-combined.

Up to this point the mind is seen to be more or less of an automatic, instinctive faculty. It may be traced from the purely reflex activity of the lowest forms of life up through the lower animals, step by step, until a very high degree of mental power is perceived in animals like the horse, dog, or elephant. But there is something lacking. There is missing that peculiar power of thinking in symbols and abstract conceptions which distinguishes the human race and which is closely bound up with the faculty of language or expressing thoughts in words. The comparatively high mental process of the lower animals is dwarfed by the human faculty of "thinking." And *thinking* is the manifestation of the intellect.

What is it to *think*? Strange to say, very few persons can answer this question correctly at first. They find themselves inclined to answer the inquiry in the words of the child: "Why, to think is to *think*!" Let us see if we can make it plain. The dictionary definition is a little too technical to be of much use to the beginner, but here it is: "To employ any of the intellectual powers except that of simple perception through the senses." But what are the "intellectual powers" so employed, and how are they employed? Let us see.

Stating the matter plainly in common terms, we may say that "thinking" is the mental process of (1) comparing our perceptions of things with each other, noting the points of likeness and of difference; (2) classifying them according to the ascertained likeness or difference, and thus tying them up in mental bundles with each set of "things of a kind" in its own bundle; (3) forming the abstract, symbolic mental idea (concept) of each class of things, so grouped, which we may afterward use as we use figures in mathematical calculations; (4) using these concepts in order to form *inferences*, that is, to reason from the known to the unknown, and to form judgments regarding things; (5) comparing these judgments and deducing higher judgments from them; and so on.

Without thinking, man would be dependent upon each particular experience for his knowledge, except so far as memory and imagination could instinctively aid him. By thought processes he is enabled to infer that if certain things be true of one of a certain kind of things, the same thing may be expected from others of the same class. As he is able to note points of likeness or difference, he is able to form clearer and truer inferences. In addition, he is able to apply his constructive imagination to the rearrangement and recombination of things whose nature he has discovered, and thus progress along the line of material achievement as well as of knowledge. It must be remembered, however, that the intellect depends entirely for its material upon the perception, which in turn receives its raw material from the senses. The intellect merely groups together the material of perception, makes inferences, draws conclusions from, and forms conclusions regarding, them, and in the case of constructive imagination recombines them in effective forms and arrangement. The intellect is the last in order in the course of mental evolution. It appears last in order in the mind of the child, but it often persists in old age after the feelings have grown dim and the memory weak.

Concepts

What is known as the "concept" is the first fruit of the elemental processes of thought. The various images of outside objects are sensed, then perceived, and then grouped according to their likenesses and differences, and the result is the production of concepts. It is difficult to define a concept so as to convey any meaning to the beginner. For instance, the dictionaries give the definition as "an abstract, general conception, idea, or notion formed in the mind." Not very clear this, is it? Perhaps we can understand it better if we say that the terms dog, cat, man, horse, house, etc., each expresses a concept. Every term expresses a concept; every general name of a thing or quality is a term applied to the concept. We shall see this a little clearer as we proceed.

We form a concept in this way: (1) We *perceive* a number of things; (2) then we notice certain *qualities* possessed by things—certain properties, attributes, or characteristics which make the thing what it is; (3) then we *compare* these qualities of the thing with the qualities of other things and see that there is a likeness in some cases, in various degrees, and a difference in other cases, in various degrees; (4) then we *generalize* or *classify* the perceived things according to their ascertained likenesses and differences; (5) then we form a *general idea* or *concept* embodying each class of thing; and, finally, we give to the concept a *term*, or *name*, which is its symbol.

The concept is a *general idea* of a class of things; the *term* is the expression of that general idea. The concept is the idea of a class of things; the term is the *label* affixed to the thing. To illustrate this last distinction, let us take the concept and term of "bird," for instance. By perception, comparison, and classification of the qualities of living things we have arrived at the conclusion that there exists a great general class the qualities of which may be stated thus: "Warm-blooded, feathered, winged, oviparous, vertebrate." To this general class of quality-possessing animals we apply the English term "bird." The name is merely a symbol. In German the term is *vogel*; in Latin, *avis*; but in each and every case the *general idea* or *concept* above stated, *i.e.*, "warm-blooded, feathered, winged, oviparous, vertebrate," is meant. If anything is found having all of those particular qualities, then we know it must be what we call a "bird." And everything that we call a "bird" must have those qualities. The term "bird" is the symbol for that particular combination of qualities existing in a thing.

There is a difference between a mental image of the imagination and a concept. The mental image must always be of a *particular* thing, while the concept is always an idea of a *general class* of things which cannot be clearly pictured in the mind. For instance, the imagination may form the mental picture of any known bird, or even of an imaginary bird, but that bird always will be a distinct, *particular* bird. Try to form a mental picture of the general class of birds—how will you do it? Do you realize the difficulty? First, such an image would have to include the characteristics of the large birds, such as the eagle, ostrich, and condor; and of the small birds, such as the wren and humming bird. It must be a composite of the shape of all birds, from the ostrich, swan, eagle, crane, down to the sparrow, swallow, and humming bird. It must picture the particular qualities of birds of prey, water birds, and domestic fowls, as well as the grain eaters.

It must exhibit all the colors found in bird life, from the brightest reds and greens down to the sober grays and browns. A little thought will show that a clear mental image of such a concept is impossible. What the most of us do, when we think of "bird," is to picture a vague, flying shape of dull color; but when we stop to think that the term must also include the waddling duck and the scratching barnyard chicken, we see that our mental image is faulty.

The trouble is that the term "bird" really means "all-bird," and we cannot picture an "all-bird" from the very nature of the case. Our terms, therefore, are like mathematical figures, or algebraic symbols, which we use for ease, speed, and clearness of thinking.

The trouble does not end here. Concepts not only include the general idea of *things*, but also the general idea of the *qualities of things*. Thus sweetness, hardness, courage, and energy are concepts, but we cannot form a mental image of them by themselves.

We may picture a sweet *thing*, but not sweetness itself. So you see that a concept is a purely abstract mental idea—a symbol—akin to the figures 1, 2, 3, etc., and used in the same way. They *stand* for general classes of things. A "term" is the verbal and written expression of the general idea or concept. The student is requested to fix these distinctions in his mind, so as to render further understanding of them easy.

21
Conception

THE process of conception has been well defined by Gordy as "that act of mind by which it forms an idea of a class; or that act of the mind that enables us to use general names intelligently." He adds: "It is, of course, understood that I am using the word 'class' to denote an indefinite number of individuals that resemble each other in certain particulars."

Perception

The first step in conception, as we have seen, is that of perception. It is readily perceived that the character of our intellectual processes depends materially upon the variety, clearness, and accuracy of our perceptions. Therefore, again, we would refer our students to the chapter in which we have stated the importance of clear perception.

Memory

The future steps of conception depend materially upon the clearness of the memory, as we can classify objects only by remembering their qualities beyond the immediate moment of actual, original perception. Therefore, the memory should be strengthened for this as well as other objects.

Abstraction

The second step in conception is that of the mental abstraction of qualities from the observed thing. That is, we must perceive and then mentally *set aside* the observed qualities of the thing. For instance, man first perceived the existence of certain qualities in things. He found that a certain number of things possessed some of these qualities in common, while others possessed other qualities in the same way, and thus arose classification from comparison. But both comparison and classification are possible only by abstraction, or *the perception of the quality as a "thing"*; thus, the abstraction of the idea of the quality of *sweetness* from the idea of sugar. Sweetness is a *quality* rather than a thing itself. It is something possessed by sugar which helps to make sugar what it is.

Color, shape, size, mental qualities, habits of action—these are some of the qualities first observed in things and abstracted from them in thought. Redness, sweetness, hardness, softness, largeness, smallness, fragrance, swiftness, slowness, fierceness, gentleness, warmness, coldness, etc.—these are abstracted qualities of things. Of course these qualities are really never divorced from things, but the mind divorces them in order to make thinking easier. An authority says: "Animals are incapable of making abstractions, and that is the reason why they cannot develop formal thought.

* * *

Abstract thought is identical with rational thought, which is the characteristic feature of the thought of speaking beings. This is the reason why abstract thought is upon earth the exclusive property of man, and why brutes are incapable of abstract thought. The process of naming is the mechanism of abstraction, for names establish the mental independence of the objects named."

The processes of abstraction depend upon attention—concentrated attention. Attention directed to the qualities of a thing tends to abstract the qualities in thought from the thing itself. Mill says: "Abstraction is primarily the result of attention." Hamilton says: "Attention and abstraction are only the same process viewed in different relations." Cultivation of the power of abstraction means principally cultivation of attention. Any mental activity which tends toward *analysis* or separation of a thing into its parts, qualities, or elements will serve to cultivate and develop the power of abstraction.

The habit of converting *qualities* into concepts is acquired by *transforming adjective terms into their corresponding noun terms*. For instance, a piece of colored candy possesses the *qualities* of being round, hard, red, sweet, etc. Transforming these adjective qualities into noun terms we have the *concepts* of roundness, hardness, redness, and sweetness, respectively.

Comparison

The third step in conception is that of *comparison*, in which the qualities of several things are compared or examined for likenesses and differences. We find many qualities in which the several things differ, and a few in which there is a likeness. Classes are formed from resemblances or likenesses, while individuals are separated from apparent classes by detection of differences. Finally, it is found that separate things, while having many points of difference which indicate their individuality, nevertheless have a few points of likeness which indicate that they belong to the same general family or class. The detection of likenesses and differences in the qualities of various things is an important mental process. Many of the higher thought processes depend largely upon the ability to compare things properly. The development of attention and perception tends to develop the power of comparison.

Classification or Generalization

The fourth step in conception is that of classification or generalization, whereby we place individual things in a mental bundle or class, and then this bundle in company with other bundles into a higher class, and so on. Thus we group all the individual small birds having certain characteristics into a species, then several related species into a larger family, and this into a still larger, until finally we group all the bird families into the great family which we call "birds" and of which the simple term "bird" expresses the general concept.

Jevons says: "We classify things together whenever we observe that they are like each other in any respect, and therefore think of them together. In classifying a collection of objects, we do not merely put together into groups those which resemble each other, but we also divide each class into smaller ones in which the resemblance is more complete. Thus the class of *white substances* may be divided into those which are solid, and those which are fluid, so that we get the two minor classes of solid-white and fluid-white substances. It is desirable to have names by which to show that one class is contained in another, and, accordingly, we call the class which is divided into two or more smaller ones the *genus*, and the smaller ones into which it is divided, the *species*."

Every *species* is a small family of the individuals composing it, and at the same time is an individual species of the genus just above it; the *genus*, in turn, is a family of several species, and at the same time an individual genus in the greater family or genus above it.

The student may familiarize himself with the idea of generalization by considering himself as an individual, John Smith. John represents that unit of generalization. The next step is to combine John with the other Smiths of his immediate family. Then this family may be grouped with his near blood relations, and so on, until finally all the related Smiths, near and remote, are grouped together in a great Smith family.

Or, in the same way, the family group may be enlarged until it takes in all the white people in a county, then all the white people in the state, then all in the United States; then all the white races, then all the white and other light-skinned races, then all mankind. Then, if one is inclined, the process may be continued until it embraces every living creature from moneron to man. Reversing the process, living creatures may be divided and subdivided until all mankind is seen to stand as a class. Then the race of man may be divided into sub-races according to color; then the white race may be subdivided into Americans and non-Americans. Then the Americans may be divided into inhabitants of the several states, or into Indianans and non-Indianans; then into the inhabitants of the several counties of Indiana, and thus the Posey Countians are reached. Then the Posey County people are divided into Smiths and non-Smiths; then the Smith family into its constituent family groups, and then into the smaller families, and so on, until the classification reaches one particular John Smith, who at last is found to be an individual—in a class by himself. This is the story of the ascending and descending processes of generalization.

22

Classes Of Concepts

IN the preceding chapter we have seen the process of conception—of the forming of concepts. *The idea of a general class of things or qualities is a concept.* Each concept contains the qualities which are *common to all* the individuals composing the class, but not those qualities which pertain only to the minor classes or the individuals. For instance, the concept of "bird" will necessarily include the common qualities of warm-bloodedness, featheredness, wingedness, oviparousness, and vertebratedness. But it will *not* include color, special shape, size, or special features or characteristics of the subfamilies or individuals composing the great class. The class comprises the individuals and subclasses composing it; the concept includes the general and common qualities which *all* in the class possess. A *percept* is the mental image of a particular thing; a *concept* is the mental idea of the general qualities of a class of things. A percept arises from the perception of a sensation; a concept is a purely mental, abstract creation, whose only existence is in the world of ideas and which has no corresponding individual object in the world of sense.

There are two general classes of concepts, namely: (1) concrete concepts, in which the common qualities of a class of things are combined into one conceptual idea, such as "bird," of which we have spoken; (2) abstract concepts, in which is combined the idea of some *quality* common to a number of things, such as "sweetness" or "redness." Jevons's well-known rule for terms is an aid in remembering this classification: "*A concrete term is the name of a thing; an abstract term is the name of a quality of a thing.*"

It is a peculiar fact and rule of concrete concepts that (1) the larger the class of things embraced in a concept, the smaller are its general qualities; and (2) the larger the number of general qualities included in a concept, the smaller the number of individuals embraced by it. For instance, the term "bird" embraces a great number of individuals—all the birds that are in existence, in fact, but it has but few general qualities, as we have seen. On the contrary, the concept "stork" has a much larger number of general qualities, but embraces far fewer individuals. Finally, the individual is reached, and we find that it has more qualities than any class can have; but it is composed of the smallest possible number of individuals, one. The secret is this: No two individuals can have as many qualities *in common* as each has individually, unless they are precisely alike, which is impossible in nature.

Imperfect Concepts

It is said that outside of strictly scientific definitions very few persons agree in their concepts of the same thing. Each has his or her own concept of the particular thing which he or she expresses by the same term. A number of persons asked to define a common term like "love," "religion," "faith," "belief," etc., will give such a variety of answers as to cause wonderment. As Green says: "My idea or image is mine alone—the reward of careless observation if imperfect; of attentive, careful, and varied observation if correct. Between mine and yours a great gulf is fixed. No man can pass from mine to yours, or from yours to mine. Neither in any proper sense of the term can mine be conveyed to you. Words do not convey thoughts; they are not vehicles of thoughts in any true sense of that term. A word is simply a common symbol which each associates with his own idea or image."

The reason of the difference in the concepts of several persons is that very few of our concepts are nearly perfect; the majority of them are quite imperfect and incomplete. Jevons gives us an idea of this in his remarks on classification: "Things may seem to be very much like each other which are not so. Whales, porpoises, seals, and several other animals live in the sea exactly like a fish; they have a similar shape and are usually classed among fish. People are said to go whale fishing. Yet these animals are not really fish at all, but are much more like dogs and horses and other quadrupeds than they are like fish. They cannot live entirely under water and breathe the air contained in the water like fish, but they have to come to the surface at intervals to take breath. Similarly, we must not class bats with birds because they fly about, although they have what would be called wings; these wings are not like those of birds, and, in truth, bats are much more like rats and mice than they are like birds. Botanists used at one time to classify plants according to their size, as trees, shrubs, or herbs, but we now know that a great tree is often more similar in character to a tiny herb than it is to other great trees. A daisy has little resemblance to a great Scotch thistle; yet the botanist regards them as very similar. The lofty growing bamboo is a kind of grass, and the sugar cane also belongs to the same class with wheat and oats."

It is a matter of importance that clear concepts should be formed regarding at least the familiar things of life. The list of clear concepts should be added to from time to time by study, investigation, and examination.

The dictionary should be consulted frequently, and a term studied until one has a clear meaning of the concept the term seeks to express.

A good encyclopedia (not necessarily an expensive one, in these days of cheap editions) will also prove very useful in this respect. As Halleck says: "It must be borne in mind that most of our concepts are subject to change during our entire life; that at first they are made only in a tentative way; that experience may show us, at any time, that they have been erroneously formed, that we have abstracted too little or too much, made the class too wide or too narrow, or that here a quality must be added or there one taken away."

It is a good practice to make a memorandum of anything of which you may hear, but of which you know nothing, and then later to make a brief but thorough investigation of that thing, by means of the dictionary and encyclopedia, and of whatever good works may be obtained on the subject, not leaving it until you feel that you have obtained at least a *clear idea* of what the thing really *means*.

A half hour each evening devoted to exercise of this kind will result in a wonderful increase of general information. We have heard of a man who made a practice of reading a short article in the encyclopedia every evening, giving preference to subjects generally classed as familiar.

In a year he made a noticeable advance in general knowledge as well as habits of thought. In five years he was looked upon by his associates as a man of a remarkably large field of general information and of more than ordinary intelligence, which verdict was a just one. As a rule we waste far more time on worthless fiction than we are willing to devote to a little self-improvement of this kind. We shrink at the idea of a general course of instructive reading, little realizing that we can take our study in small installments and at a very little cost in time or labor.

Our concepts form the material which our intellect uses in its reasoning processes. No matter how good a reasoner one may be, unless he has a good supply of general information about the things of which he is reasoning, he will not make much real headway. We must begin at the bottom and build a firm foundation upon which the intellectual structure may be erected. This foundation is composed of *facts*. These facts are represented by our clear and correct concepts.

23
Judgments

WE have seen the several steps of the mental process whereby simple sensations are transformed into percepts and then into concepts or general ideas. The formation of the concept is considered as the first great step in thinking. The second great step in thinking is that of the formation of the "judgment." The definition of "judgment," as the term is used in logic; is "the comparing together in the mind of two ideas of things, and determining whether they agree or disagree with each other, or that one of them does or does not belong to the other. Judgment is, therefore, (*a*) affirmative or (*b*) negative, as (*a*) 'Snow is white,' or (*b*) 'All white men are not Europeans.'"

What in logic is called a "proposition" is the expression in words of a logical judgment. Hyslop defined the term "proposition" as follows: "Any affirmation or denial of an agreement between two conceptions." For instance, we compare the concepts "sparrow" and "bird" and find that there is an agreement, and that the former belongs to the latter; this mental process is a *judgment*. We then announce the judgment in the *proposition*: "The sparrow is a bird." In the same way we compare the concepts "bat" and "bird," find that there is a disagreement, and form the judgment that neither belongs to the other, which we express in the proposition: "The bat is not a bird." Or we may form the judgment that "sweetness" is a quality of "sugar," which we express in the proposition: "Sugar is sweet." Likewise, we may form the judgment which results in the proposition: "Vinegar is not sweet."

While the process of judgment is generally considered as constituting the second great step of thinking, coming after the formation of the concept, and consisting of the comparing of concepts, it must be remembered that the act of judging is far more elementary than this, for it is found still farther back in the history of thought processes. By that peculiar law of paradox which we find everywhere operative in mind processes, the same process of forming judgments which is used in comparing concepts also has been used in forming the same concepts in the stage of comparison. In fact, the result of all comparison, high or low, must be *a judgment.*

Halleck says: "Judgment is necessary in forming concepts. When we decide that a quality is or is not common to a class, we are really judging. This is another evidence of the complexity and unified action of the mind." Brooks says: "The power of judgment is of great value in its products. It is involved in or accompanies every act of the intellect, and thus lies at the foundation of all intellectual activity. It operates directly in every act of the understanding, and even aids the other faculties of the mind in completing their activities and products.

* * *

Strictly speaking, every intelligent act of the mind is accompanied with a judgment. To know is to discriminate and, therefore, to judge. Every sensation or cognition involves a knowledge and so a judgment that it exists. The mind cannot think at all without judging; to think is to judge. Even in forming the notions which judgment compares, the mind judges. Every notion or concept implies a previous act of judgment to form it; in forming a concept we compare the common attributes before we unite them, and comparison is judgment. It is thus true that 'Every concept is a contracted judgment; every judgment an expanded concept.'"

It is needless to say that as judgments lie at the base of our thinking, and also appear in every part of its higher structure, the importance of correct judgment in thought cannot be overestimated. But it is often very difficult to form correct judgment even regarding the most familiar things around us. Halleck says: "In actual life things present themselves to us with their qualities disguised or obscured by other conflicting qualities. Men had for ages seen burning substances and had formed a concept of them. A certain hard, black, stony substance had often been noticed, and a concept had been formed of it. This concept was imperfect; but it is very seldom that we meet with perfect, sharply-defined concepts in actual life. So it happened that for ages the concept of burning substance was never linked by judgment to the concept of stone coal. The combustible quality in the coal was overshadowed by its stony attributes. 'Of course stone will not burn,' people said. One cannot tell how long the development of mankind was retarded for that very reason. England would not to-day be manufacturing products for the rest of the world had not some one judged coal to be a combustible substance.

* * *

Judgment is ever silently working and comparing things that to past ages seemed dissimilar; and it is constantly abstracting and leaving out of the field of view those qualities which have simply served to obscure the point at issue."

Gordy says: "The credulity of children is proverbial; but if we get our facts at first hand, if we study 'the living, learning, playing child,' we shall see that he is quite as remarkable for incredulity as for credulity. The explanation is simple: *He tends to believe the first suggestion that comes into his mind, no matter from what source*; and since his belief is not the result of any rational process, he cannot be made to disbelieve it in any rational way. Hence it is that he is very credulous about any matter about which he has no ideas; but let the idea once get possession of his mind, and he is quite as remarkable for incredulity as before for credulity.

* * *

If we study the larger child,—the man with a child's mind, an uneducated man,—we shall have the same truth forced upon us. If the beliefs of men were due to processes of reasoning, where they have not reasoned they would not believe. But do we find it so? Is it not true that the men who have the most positive opinions on the largest variety of subjects—so far as they have ever heard of them—are precisely those who have the least right to them? Socrates, we remember, was counted the wisest man in Athens because he alone resisted his natural tendency to believe in the absence of evidence; he alone would not delude himself with the conceit of knowledge without the reality; and it would scarcely be too much to say that the intellectual strength of men is in direct proportion to the number of things they are absolutely certain of.

* * *

I do not, of course, mean to intimate that we should have no opinions about matters that we have not personally investigated. We take, and ought to take, the opinion of some men about law, and others about medicine, and others about particular sciences, and so on. But we should clearly realize the difference between holding an opinion on trust and holding it as the result of our own investigations."

Brooks says: "It should be one of the leading objects of the culture of young people to lead them to acquire the habit of forming judgments. They should not only be led to see things but to have opinions about things. They should be trained to see things in their relations and to put these relations into definite propositions. Their ideas of objects should be worked up into thoughts concerning the objects. Those methods of teaching are best which tend to excite a thoughtful habit of mind that notices the similitudes and diversities of objects and endeavors to read the thoughts which they embody and of which they are the symbols."

The study of logic, geometry, and the natural sciences is recommended for exercise of the faculty of judgment and the development thereof. The study and practice of even the lower branches of mathematics are also helpful in this direction. The game of checkers or chess is recommended by many authorities. Some have advocated the practice of solving enigmas, problems, rebuses, etc., as giving exercise to this faculty of the mind. The cultivation of the "Why?" attitude of mind, and the answering of one's own mental questions, is also helpful, if not carried to excess. "Doubting Thomas" is not always a term of reproach in these days of scientific habits of thought, and "the man from Missouri" has many warm admirers.

24
Primary Laws Of Thought

IN connection with this subject we herewith call the attention of the student to the well-known Primary Laws of Thought which have been recognized as valid from the time of the ancient Greek logicians. These laws are self-evident, and are uncontradictable. They are axiomatic. Jevons says of them: "Students are seldom able to see at first their full meaning and importance. All arguments may be explained when these self-evident laws are granted; and it is not too much to say that the whole of logic will be plain to those who will constantly use these laws as their key." Here are the Three Primary Laws of Thought:—

I. *Law of Identity.* "Whatever is, *is.*"

II. *Law of Contradiction.* "Nothing can both be and not be."

III. *Law of Excluded Middle.* "Everything must either be or not be; there is no middle course."

I. The first of these laws, called "*The Law of Identity,*" informs us that a thing is always itself, no matter under what guise or form it is perceived or may present itself. An animal is always a bird if it possesses the general characteristics of a "bird," no matter whether it exhibits the minor characteristics of an eagle, a wren, a stork, or a humming bird. In the same way a whale is a mammal because it possesses the general characteristics of a mammal notwithstanding that it swims in the water like a fish. Also, sweetness is always sweetness, whether manifested in sugar, honey, flowers, or products of coal tar. If a thing *is* that thing, then it *is,* and it cannot be logically claimed that it *is not.*

II. The second of these laws, called "*The Law of Contradiction,*" informs us that the same quality or class cannot be both affirmed and denied of a thing at the same time and place. A sparrow cannot be said to be both "bird" and "not bird" at the same time. Neither can sugar be said to be "sweet" and "not sweet" at the same time. A piece of iron may be "hot" at one end and "not hot" at another, but it cannot be both "hot" and "not hot" at the same place at the same time.

III. The third of these laws, called "*The Law of Excluded Middle*," informs us that a given quality or class *must* be affirmed or denied to *everything* at any given time and place. Everything either must be of a certain class or not, must possess a certain quality or not, at a given time or place. There is no other alternative or middle course. It is axiomatic that any statement *must* either be or not be true of a certain other thing at any certain time and place; there is no escape from this. Anything *either* must be "black" or "not black," a bird or not a bird, alive or not alive, at any certain time or place. There is nothing else that it can be; it cannot both be and not be at the same time and place, as we have seen; therefore, it must either be or not be that which is asserted of it. The judgment must decide which alternative; but it has only two possible choices.

But the student must not confuse opposite qualities or things with "not-ness." A thing may be "black" or "not black," but it need not be white to be "not black," for blue is likewise "not black" just as it is "not white." The neglect of this fact frequently causes error. We must always affirm either the existence or non-existence of a quality in a thing; but this is far different from affirming or denying the existence of the opposite quality. Thus a thing may be "not hard" and yet it does not follow that it is "soft"; it may be *neither* hard nor soft.

Fallacious Application

There exists what are known as "fallacies" of application of these primary laws. A fallacy is an unsound argument or conclusion. For instance, because a particular man is found to be a liar, it is fallacious to assume that "*all* men are liars," for lying is a particular quality of the individual man, and not a general quality of the family of men. In the same way because a stork has long legs and a long bill, it does not follow that all birds must have these characteristics simply because the stork is a bird. *It is fallacious to extend an individual quality to a class.* But it is sound judgment to assume that a class quality must be possessed by all individuals in that class. It is a far different proposition which asserts that "*some* birds are black," from that which asserts that "*all* birds are black." The same rule, of course, is true regarding negative propositions.

Another fallacy is that which assumes that because the affirmative or negative proposition has not been, or cannot be, proved, it follows that the opposite proposition must be true. The true judgment is simply "not proven."

Another fallacious judgment is that which is based on attributing absolute quality to that which is but relative or comparative. For instance, the terms "hot" and "cold" are relative and comparative, and simply denote one's relative opinion regarding a fixed and certain degree of temperature. The *certain* thing is the degree of temperature, say 75 degrees Fahrenheit; of this we may logically claim that it *is* or *is not* true at a certain time or place. It either *is* 75 degrees Fahrenheit or it *is not*. But to one man this may seem *warm* and to another *cold*; both are right in their judgments, so far as their own relative feelings are concerned. But neither can claim absolutely that it is *warm* or *cold*. Therefore, it is a fallacy to ascribe absolute quality to a relative one. The *absolute fact* comes under the Law of Excluded Middle, but a personal opinion is not an absolute fact.

There are other fallacies which will be considered in other chapters of this book, under their appropriate heading.

25
Reasoning

REASONING, the third great step in thinking, may be said to consist of ascertaining new truths from old ones, new judgments from old ones, unknown facts from known ones; in short, of proceeding logically from the known to the unknown, using the known as the foundation for the unknown which is sought to be known. Gordy gives us the following excellent definition of the term: "Reasoning is the act of going from the known to the unknown through other beliefs; of basing judgment upon judgments; reaching beliefs through beliefs." Reasoning, then, is seen to be a process of building a structure of judgments, one resting upon the other, the topmost point being the final judgment, but the whole constituting an edifice of judgment. This may be seen more clearly when the various forms of reasoning are considered.

Immediate Reasoning

The simplest form of reasoning is that known as "immediate reasoning," by which is meant reasoning by directly comparing two judgments without the intervention of the third judgment, which is found in the more formal classes of reasoning. This form of reasoning depends largely upon the application of the Three Primary Laws of Thought, to which we have referred in a previous chapter.

It will be seen that *if* (*a*) a thing is always itself, then (*b*) all that is included in it must partake of its nature. Thus, the bird family has certain class characteristics, therefore by immediate reasoning we know that *any* member of that family must possess those class characteristics, whatever particular characteristics it may have in addition. And we likewise know that we cannot attribute the *particular* characteristics, as a matter of course, to the other members of the class. Thus, though all sparrows are birds, it is not true that all birds are sparrows. "All biscuits are bread; but all bread is not biscuit."

In the same way we know that a thing cannot be bird and mammal at the same time, for the mammals form a not-bird family. And, likewise, we know that everything *must* be either bird or not bird, but that being not bird does not mean being a mammal, for there are many other not-bird things than mammals. In this form of reasoning distinction is always made between the *universal* or general class, which is expressed by the word *all*, and the *particular* or individual, which is expressed by the word "some." Many persons fail to note this difference in their reasoning, and fallaciously reason, for instance, that because *some* swans are white, *all* swans must be so, which is a far different thing from reasoning that if *all* is so and so, then *some* must be so and so. Those who are interested in this subject are referred to some elementary text-book on logic, as the detailed consideration is too technical for consideration here.

Reasoning by Analogy

Reasoning by analogy is an elementary form of reasoning, and is the particular kind of reasoning employed by the majority of persons in ordinary thought. It is based upon the unconscious recognition by the human mind of the principle which is expressed by Jevons as: "*If two or more things resemble each other in many points, they will probably resemble each other in more points.*" The same authority says: "Reasoning by analogy differs only in degree from that kind of reasoning called '*generalization.*' When *many things* resemble each other in a *few properties*, we argue about them by generalization. When a *few things* resemble each other in *many properties*, it is a case of analogy."

While this form of reason is frequently employed with more or less satisfactory results, it is always open to a large percentage of error. Thus, persons have been poisoned by toadstools by reason of false analogous reasoning that because mushrooms are edible, then toadstools, which resemble them, must also be fit for food; or, in the same way, because certain berries resemble other edible berries they must likewise be good food. As Brooks says: "To infer that because John Smith has a red nose and is also a drunkard, then Henry Jones, who also has a red nose, is also a drunkard, would be dangerous inference. Conclusions of this kind drawn from analogy are frequently dangerous." Halleck says: "Many false analogies are manufactured, and it is excellent thought training to expose them. The majority of people think so little that they swallow these false analogies just as newly-fledged robins swallow small stones dropped into their mouths."

Jevons, one of the best authorities on the subject, says: "There is no way in which we can really assure ourselves that we are arguing safely by analogy. The only rule that can be given is this: That the more closely two things resemble each other, the more likely it is that they are the same in other respects, especially in points closely connected with those observed. In order to be clear about our conclusions, we ought, in fact, never to rest satisfied with mere analogy, but ought to try to discover the general laws governing the case.

* * *

We find that reasoning by analogy is not to be depended upon, unless we make such an inquiry into the causes and laws of the things in question that we really employ inductive and deductive reasoning."

Higher Forms of Reasoning

The two higher forms of reasoning are known, respectively, as (1) inductive reasoning, or inference from particular facts to general laws; and (2) deductive reasoning, or inference from general truths to particular truths. While the class distinction is made for the purpose of clear consideration, it must not be forgotten that the two forms of reasoning are generally found in combination. Thus, in inductive reasoning many steps are taken by the aid of deductive reasoning; and, likewise, before we can reason deductively from general truths to particular ones we must have discovered the general truths by inductive reasoning from particular facts. Thus there is a unity in all reasoning processes as there is in all mental operations. Inductive reasoning is a *synthetical* process; deductive reasoning, an *analytical* one. In the first we combine and build up, in the latter we dissect and separate.

26
Inductive Reasoning

INDUCTIVE reasoning is based upon the axiom: "*What is true of the many is true of the whole.*" This axiom is based upon man's belief in the uniformity of nature. Inductive reasoning is a mental ladder by which we climb from particular facts to general laws, but the ladder rests upon the belief that the universe is governed by law.

The steps in inductive reasoning are as follows:—

I. Observation, investigation, and examination of particular facts or things. If we wish to know the general characteristics of the bird family, we must first examine a sufficient number of birds of many kinds so as to discover the comparatively few general characteristics possessed by *all* of the bird family, as distinct from the particular characteristics possessed by only *some* of that family. The greater the number of individuals examined, the narrower becomes our list of the general qualities common to *all*. In the same way we must examine many kinds of flowers before we come to the few general qualities common to all flowers, which we combine in the general concept of "flower." The same, of course, is true regarding the discovery of general laws from particular facts. We examine the facts and then work toward a general law which will explain them. For instance, the Law of Gravitation was discovered by the observation and investigation of the fact that all objects are attracted to the earth; further investigation revealed the fact that all material objects are attracted to each other; then the general law was discovered, or, rather, the hypothesis was advanced, was found to explain the facts, and was verified by further experiments and observation.

II. The second step in inductive reasoning is the making of an hypothesis. An hypothesis is a proposition or principle assumed as a *possible* explanation for a set or class of facts. It is regarded as a "working theory," which must be examined and tested in connection with the facts before it is finally accepted. For instance, after the observation that a number of magnets attracted steel, it was found reasonable to advance the hypothesis that "all magnets attract steel." In the same way was advanced the hypothesis that "all birds are warm-blooded, winged, feathered, oviparous vertebrates." Subsequent observation and experiment established the hypothesis regarding the magnet, and regarding the general qualities of the bird family. If a single magnet had been found which did not attract steel, then the hypothesis would have fallen. If a single bird had been discovered which was not warm-blooded, then that quality would have been stricken from the list of the necessary characteristics of all birds.

A theory is merely an hypothesis which has been verified or established by continued and repeated observation, investigation, and experiment.

Hypotheses and theories arise very frequently from the subconscious assimilation of a number of particular facts and the consequent flashing of a "great guess," or "sacred suspicion of the truth," into the conscious field of attention. The scientific imagination plays an important part in this process. There is, of course, a world of difference between a "blind guess" based upon insufficient data and a "scientific guess" resulting from the accumulation of a vast store of careful and accurate information. As Brooks says: "The forming of an hypothesis requires a suggestive mind, a lively fancy, a philosophic imagination that catches a glimpse of the idea through the form or sees the law standing behind the fact." But accepted theories, in the majority of cases, arise only by testing out and rejecting many promising hypotheses and finally settling upon the one which best answers all the requirements and best explains the facts. As an authority says: "To try wrong guesses is with most persons the only way to hit upon right ones."

III. Testing the hypothesis by deductive reasoning is the third step in inductive reasoning. This test is made by applying the hypothetical principle to particular facts or things; that is, to follow out mentally the hypothetical principle to its logical conclusion. This may be done in this way: "If *so and so* is correct, then it follows that *thus and so* is true," etc. If the conclusion agrees with reason, then the test is deemed satisfactory so far as it has gone. But if the result proves to be a logical absurdity or inconsistent with natural facts, then the hypothesis is discredited.

IV. Practical verification of the hypothesis is the fourth step in inductive reasoning. This step consists of the actual comparison of observed facts with the "logical conclusions" arising from applying deductive reasoning to the general principle assumed as a premise. The greater number of facts agreeing with the conclusions arising from the premise of the hypothesis, the greater is deemed the "probability" of the latter. The authorities generally assume an hypothesis to be *verified* when it accounts for *all* the facts which properly are related to it. Some extremists contend, however, that before an hypothesis may be considered as absolutely verified, it must not only account for all the associated facts but that also there must be no other possible hypothesis to account for the same facts. The "facts" referred to in this connection may be either (1) observed phenomena, or (2) the conclusions of deductive reasoning arising from the assumption of the hypothesis, or (3) the agreement between the observed facts and the logical conclusions. The last combination is generally regarded as the most logical. The verification of an hypothesis must be "an all-around one," and there must be an agreement between the observed facts and the logical conclusions in the case—the hypothesis must "fit" the facts, and the facts must "fit" the hypothesis. The "facts" are the glass slipper of the Cinderella legend—the several sisters of Cinderella were discarded hypotheses, the slipper and the sisters not "fitting." When Cinderella's foot was found to be the one foot upon which the glass slipper fitted, then the Cinderella hypothesis was considered to have been proved—the glass slipper was hers and the prince claimed his bride.

27

Deductive Reasoning

WE have seen in the preceding chapter that from particular facts we reason inductively to general principles or truths. We have also seen that one of the steps of inductive reasoning is the testing of the hypothesis by deductive reasoning. We shall now also see that the results of inductive reasoning are used as premises or bases for deductive reasoning. These two forms of reasoning are opposites and yet complementary to each other; they are in a sense independent and yet are interdependent. Brooks says: "The two methods of reasoning are the reverse of each other. One goes from particulars to generals; the other from generals to particulars. One is a process of analysis; the other is a process of synthesis. One rises from facts to laws; the other descends from laws to facts. Each is independent of the other, and each is a valid and essential method of inference."

Halleck well expresses the spirit of deductive reasoning as follows: "After induction has classified certain phenomena and thus given us a major premise, we may proceed deductively to apply the inference to any new specimen that can be shown to belong to that class. Induction hands over to deduction a ready-made premise. Deduction takes that as a fact, making no inquiry regarding its truth. Only after general laws have been laid down, after objects have been classified, after major premises have been formed, can deduction be employed."

Deductive reasoning proceeds from general principles to particular facts. It is a descending process, analytical in its nature. It rests upon the fundamental axiomatic basis that "*whatever is true of the whole is true of its parts*," or "*whatever is true of the universal is true of the particulars*."

The process of deductive reasoning may be stated briefly as follows: (1) A general principle of a class is stated as a *major premise*; (2) a particular thing is stated as belonging to that general class, this statement being the *minor premise*; therefore (3) the general class principle is held to apply to the particular thing, this last statement being the *conclusion*. (*A "premise" is "a proposition assumed to be true."*)

The following gives us an illustration of the above process:—

I. (*Major premise*)—A bird is a warm-blooded, feathered, winged, oviparous vertebrate.

II. (*Minor premise*)—The sparrow is a bird; therefore

III. (*Conclusion*)—The sparrow is a warm-blooded, feathered, winged, oviparous vertebrate.

Or, again:—

I. (*Major premise*)—Rattlesnakes frequently bite when enraged, and their bite is poisonous.

II. (*Minor premise*)—This snake before me is a rattlesnake; therefore

III. (*Conclusion*)—This snake before me may bite when enraged, and its bite will be poisonous.

The average person may be inclined to object that he is not conscious of going through this complicated process when he reasons about sparrows or rattlesnakes. But he *does*, nevertheless. He is not conscious of the steps, because mental habit has accustomed him to the process, and it is performed more or less automatically. But these three steps manifest in all processes of deductive reasoning, even the simplest. The average person is like the character in the French play who was surprised to learn that he had "been talking prose for forty years without knowing it." Jevons says that the majority of persons are equally surprised when they find out that they have been using logical forms, more or less correctly, without having realized it. He says: "A large number even of educated persons have no clear idea of what logic is. Yet, in a certain way, every one must have been a logician since he began to speak."

There are many technical rules and principles of logic which we cannot attempt to consider here. There are, however, a few elementary principles of correct reasoning which should have a place here. What is known as a "syllogism" is the expression in words of the various parts of the complete process of reasoning or argument. Whately defines it as follows: "A syllogism is an argument expressed in strict logical form so that its conclusiveness is manifest from the structure of the expression alone, without any regard to the meaning of the term." In short, *if* the two premises are accepted as correct, it follows that there can be only one true logical conclusion resulting therefrom. In abstract or theoretical reasoning the word "*if*" is assumed to precede each of the two premises, the "therefore" before the conclusion resulting from the "if," of course. The following are the general rules governing the syllogism:—

I. Every syllogism must consist of three, and no more than three, propositions, namely (1) the major premise, (2) the minor premise, and (3) the conclusion.

II. The conclusion must naturally follow from the premises, otherwise the syllogism is invalid and constitutes a fallacy or sophism.

III. One premise, at least, must be affirmative.

IV. If one premise is negative, the conclusion must be negative.

V. One premise, at least, must be universal or general.

VI. If one premise is particular, the conclusion also must be particular.

The last two rules (V. and VI.) contain the essential principles of all the rules regarding syllogisms, and any syllogism which breaks them will be found also to break other rules, some of which are not stated here for the reason that they are too technical. These two rules may be tested by constructing syllogisms in violation of their principles. The reason for them is as follows: (Rule V.) Because "from two particular premises no conclusion can be drawn," as, for instance: (1) Some men are mortal; (2) John is a man. We cannot reason from this either that John *is* or *is not* mortal. The major premise should read "*all* men." (Rule VI.) Because "a universal conclusion can be drawn only from two universal premises," an example being needless here, as the conclusion is so obvious.

Cultivation of Reasoning Faculties

There is no royal road to the cultivation of the reasoning faculties. There is but the old familiar rule: Practice, exercise, use. Nevertheless there are certain studies which tend to develop the faculties in question. The study of arithmetic, especially mental arithmetic, tends to develop correct habits of reasoning from one truth to another—from cause to effect. Better still is the study of geometry; and best of all, of course, is the study of logic and the practice of working out its problems and examples. The study of philosophy and psychology also is useful in this way. Many lawyers and teachers have drilled themselves in geometry solely for the purpose of developing their logical reasoning powers.

Brooks says: "So valuable is geometry as a discipline that many lawyers and others review their geometry every year in order to keep the mind drilled to logical habits of thinking.

* * *

The study of logic will aid in the development of the power of deductive reasoning. It does this, first, by showing the method by which we reason. To know how we reason, to see the laws which govern the reasoning process, to analyze the syllogism and see its conformity to the laws of thought, is not only an exercise of reasoning but gives that knowledge of the process that will be both a stimulus and a guide to thought. No one can trace the principles and processes of thought without receiving thereby an impetus to thought. In the second place, the study of logic is probably even more valuable because it gives practice in deductive thinking.

This, perhaps, is its principal value, since the mind reasons instinctively without knowing how it reasons. One can think without the knowledge of the science of thinking just as one can use language correctly without a knowledge of grammar; yet as the study of grammar improves one's speech, so the study of logic can but improve one's thought."

In the opinion of the writer hereof, one of the best though simple methods of cultivating the faculties of reasoning is to acquaint one's self thoroughly with the more common *fallacies* or forms of false reasoning—so thoroughly that not only is the false reasoning detected at once but also the *reason* of its falsity is readily understood. To understand the wrong ways of reasoning is to be on guard against them.

By guarding against them we tend to eliminate them from our thought processes. If we eliminate the false we have the true left in its place. Therefore we recommend the weeding of the logical garden of the common fallacies, to the end that the flowers of pure reason may flourish in their stead. Accordingly, we think it well to call your attention in the next chapter to the more common fallacies, and the reason of their falsity.

28
Fallacious Reasoning

FALLACY is defined as "an unsound argument or mode of arguing which, while appearing to be decisive of a question, is in reality not so; or a fallacious statement or proposition in which the error is not readily apparent. When a fallacy is used to deceive others, it is called 'sophistry,'" It is important that the student should understand the nature of the fallacy and understand its most common forms. As Jevons says: "In learning how to do right it is always desirable to be informed as to the ways in which we are likely to go wrong. In describing to a man the road which he should follow, we ought to tell him not only the turnings which he is to take but also the turnings which he is to avoid. Similarly, it is a useful part of logic which teaches us the ways and turnings by which people most commonly go astray in reasoning."

In presenting the following brief statement regarding the more common forms of fallacy, we omit so far as possible the technical details which belong to text-books on logic.

Fallacies

I. *True Collective but False Particular.*—An example of this fallacy is found in the argument that because the French race, collectively, are excitable, therefore a particular Frenchman must be excitable. Or that because the Jewish race, collectively, are good business people, therefore the particular Jew must be a good business man. This is as fallacious as arguing that because a man may drown in the ocean he should avoid the bath, basin, or cup of water. There is a vast difference between the whole of a thing and its separate parts. Nitric acid and glycerin, separately, are not explosive, but, combined, they form nitro-glycerin, a most dangerous and powerful explosive. Reversing this form of illustration, we remind you of the old saying: "Salt is a good thing; but one doesn't want to be put in pickle."

II. *Irrelevant Conclusion.*—This fallacy consists in introducing in the conclusion matter not contained in the premises, or in the confusing of the issue. For instance: (1) All men are sinful; (2) John Smith is a man; therefore (3) John Smith is a horse thief. This may sound absurd, but many arguments are as fallacious as this, and for the same reason. Or another and more subtle form: (1) All thieves are liars; (2) John Smith is a liar; therefore (3) John Smith is a thief. The first example arises from the introduction of new matter, and the last from the confusion of the issue.

III. *False Cause.*—This fallacy consists in attributing cause to a thing which is merely coincident with, or precedent to, the effect. For instance: (1) The cock crows just before or at the moment of sunrise; therefore (2) the cock-crowing is the cause of the sunrise. Or, again: (1) Bad crops followed the election of a Whig president; therefore (2) the Whig party is the cause of the bad crops. Or, again: (1) Where civilization is the highest, there we find the greatest number of high hats; therefore (2) high hats are the cause of civilization.

IV. *Circular Reasoning.*—In this form of fallacy the person reasoning or arguing endeavors to explain or prove a thing by itself or its own terms. For instance: (1) The Whig party is honest because it advocates honest principles; (2) the Whig principles are honest because they are advocated by an honest party. A common form of this fallacy in its phase of sophistry is the use of synonyms in such a manner that they seem to express more than the original conception, whereas they are really but other terms for the same thing. An historic example of circular reasoning is the following: (1) The Church of England is the true Church, because it was established by God; (2) it must have been established by God, because it is the true Church. This form of sophistry is most effective when employed in long arguments in which it is difficult to detect it.

V. *Begging the Question.*—This fallacy arises from the use of a false premise, or at least of a premise the truth of which is not admitted by the opponent. It may be stated, simply, as "*the unwarranted assumption of a premise, generally the major premise.*" Many persons in public life argue in this way. They boldly assert an unwarranted premise, and then proceed to argue logically from it. The result is confusing to the average person, for, the steps of the reasoning being logical, it seems as if the argument is sound, the fact of the unwarranted premise being overlooked. The person using this form of sophistry proceeds on Aaron Burr's theory of truth being "that which is boldly asserted and plausibly maintained."

Bulwer makes one of his characters mention a particularly atrocious form of this fallacy (although an amusing one) in the following words: "Whenever you are about to utter something astonishingly false, always begin with: 'It is an acknowledged fact,' etc. Sir Robert Filmer was a master of this manner of writing. Thus with what a solemn face that great man attempted to cheat. He would say: '*It is a truth undeniable* that there cannot be any multitude of men whatsoever, either great or small, etc., but that in the same multitude there is one man among them *that in nature hath a right to be King of all the rest—as being the next heir of Adam*!'"

Look carefully for the major premise of propositions advanced in argument, spoken or written. Be sure that the person making the proposition is not "begging the question" by *the unwarranted assumption of the premise.*

General Rule of Inference

Hyslop says concerning valid inferences and fallacious ones: "We cannot infer *anything* we please from any premises we please. We must conform to certain definite rules or principles. Any violation of them will be a fallacy. There are two simple rules which should not be violated: (1) *The subject-matter in the conclusion should be of the same general kind as in the premises*; (2) *the facts constituting the premises must be accepted and must not be fictitious.*" A close observance of these rules will result in the detection and avoidance of the principal forms of fallacious reasoning and sophistry.

Sophistical Arguments

There are a number of tricky practices resorted to by persons in argument, that are fallacious in intent and result, which we do not consider here in detail as they scarcely belong to the particular subject of this book. A brief mention, however, may be permitted in the interest of general information. Here are the principal ones:—

(1) Arguing that a proposition is correct because the opponent cannot prove the contrary. The fallacy is seen when we realize that the statement, "The moon is made of green cheese," is not proved because we cannot prove the contrary. No amount of failure to *disprove* a proposition really *proves* it; and no amount of failure to *prove* a proposition really *disproves* it. As a general rule, the burden of proof rests upon the person stating the proposition, and his opponent is not called upon to disprove it or else have it considered proved. The old cry of "You cannot *prove* that it is *not* so" is based upon a fallacious conception.

(2) Abuse of the opponent, his party, or his cause. This is no real argument or reasoning. It is akin to proving a point by beating the opponent over the head.

(3) Arguing that an opponent does not live up to his principles is no argument against the principles he advocates. A man may advocate the principle of temperance and yet drink to excess. This simply proves that he preaches better than he practices; but the truth of the principle of temperance is not affected in any way thereby. The proof of this is that he may change his practices; and it cannot be held that the change of his personal habits improves or changes the nature of the principle.

(4) Argument of authority is not based on logic. Authority is valuable when really worthy, and merely as corroboration or adding weight; but it is not logical argument. The *reasons* of the authority alone constitute a real argument. The abuse of this form of argument is shown, in the above reference to "begging the question," in the quotation from Bulwer.

(5) Appeal to prejudice or public opinion is not a valid argument, for public opinion is frequently wrong and prejudice is often unwarranted. And, at the best, they "have nothing to do with the case" from the standpoint of logic. The abuse of testimony and claimed evidence is also worthy of examination, but we cannot go into the subject here.

Fallacies of Prejudice

But perhaps the most dangerous of all fallacies in the search for truth on the part of the most of us are those which arise from the following:—

(1) The tendency to reason from what we feel and wish to be true, rather than from the actual facts of the case, which causes us unconsciously to assume the mental attitude of "if the facts agree with our likes and pet theories, all is well; if they do not, so much the worse for the facts."

(2) The tendency in all of us to perceive only the facts that agree with our theories and to ignore the others. We find that for which we seek, and overlook that which does not interest us. Our discoveries follow our interest, and our interest follows our desires and beliefs.

The intelligent man or woman realizes these tendencies of human nature and endeavors to avoid them in his or her own reasoning, but is keenly conscious of them in the arguments and reasoning of others. A failure to observe and guard one's self against these tendencies results in bigotry, intolerance, narrowness, and intellectual astigmatism.

29
The Will

THE activities of the will comprise the third great class of mental processes. Psychologists always have differed greatly in their conception of just what constitutes these activities. Even to-day it is difficult to obtain a dictionary definition of the will that agrees with the best opinion on the subject. The dictionaries adhere to the old classification and conception which regarded the will as "that faculty of the mind or soul by which it chooses or decides." But with the growth of the idea that the will acts according to the strongest motive, and that the motive is supplied by the average struck between the desires of the moment, under the supervision of the intellect, the conception of will as the choosing and deciding faculty is passing from favor. In the place of the older conception has come the newer one which holds that the will is primarily concerned with *action*.

It is difficult to place the will in the category of mental processes. But it is generally agreed that it abides in the very center of the mental being, and is closely associated with what is called the ego, or self. The will seems to have at least three general phases, viz.: (1) The phase of desire, (2) the phase of deliberation or choice, and (3) the phase of expression in action. In order to understand the will, it is necessary to consider each of these three phases of its activities.

(1). Desire.

The first phase of will, which is called "desire," is in itself somewhat complex. On its lower side it touches, and, in fact, blends into, feeling and emotion. Its center consists of a state of *tension*, akin to that of a coiled spring or a cat crouching ready for a spring. On its higher side it touches, penetrates, and blends into the other phases of the will which we have mentioned.

Desire is defined as "a feeling, emotion, or excitement of the mind directed toward the attainment, enjoyment, or possession of some object from which pleasure, profit, or gratification is expected." Halleck gives us the following excellent conception of the moving spirit of desire: "*Desire has for its object something which will bring pleasure or get rid of pain, immediate or remote, for the individual or for some one in whom he is interested. Aversion, or a striving away from something, is merely the negative aspect of desire.*"

In Halleck's statement, above quoted, we have the explanation of the part played by the intellect in the activities of will. The intellect is able to perceive the relations between present action and future results, and is able to point the way toward the suppression of some desires in order that other and better ones may be manifested. It also serves its purposes in regulating the "striking of the average" between conflicting desires. Without the intervention of the intellect, the temporary desire of the moment would invariably be acted upon without regard to future results or consequences to one's self and others. It also serves to point out the course of action calculated to give the most satisfactory expression of the desire.

While it is a fact that the action of will depends almost entirely upon the motive force of desire, it is likewise true that desire may be created, regulated, suppressed, and even killed by the action of the will. The will, by giving or refusing attention to a certain class of desires, may either cause them to grow and wax strong, or else die and fade away. It must be remembered, however, that this use of the will itself springs from another set of desires or feelings.

Desire is aroused by feelings or emotions rising from the subconscious planes of the mind and seeking expression and manifestation. We have considered the nature of the feelings and emotions in previous chapters, which should be read in connection with the present one. It should be remembered that the feeling or emotional side of desire arises from either inherited race memories existing as instincts, or from the memory of the past experiences of the individual. In some cases the feeling first manifests in a vague unrest caused by subconscious promptings and excitement. Then the imagination pictures the object of the feeling, or certain memory images connected with it, and the desire thus manifests on the plane of consciousness.

The entrance of the desire feeling into consciousness is accompanied by that peculiar *tension* which marks the second phase of desire. This tension, when sufficiently strong, passes into the third phase of desire, or that in which desire blends into will action. Desire in this stage makes a demand upon will for expression and action. From mere feeling, and tension of feeling, it becomes *a call to action*. But before expression and action are given to it, the second phase of will must manifest at least for a moment; this second phase is that known as deliberation, or the weighing and balancing of desires.

(2). Deliberation.

The second phase of will, known as deliberation, is more than the purely intellectual process which the term would indicate. The intellect plays an important part, it is true, but there is also an almost instinctive and automatic *weighing and balancing of desires*. There is seldom only one desire presenting its claims upon the will at any particular moment. It is true that occasionally there arises an emotional desire of such dominant power and strength that it crowds out every other claimant at the bar of deliberation. But such instances are rare, and as a rule there are a host of rival claimants, each insisting upon its rights in the matter at issue. In the man of weak or undeveloped and untrained intellect, the struggle is usually little more than a brief combat between several desires, in which *the strongest at the moment wins*. But with the development of intellect new factors arise and new forces are felt. Moreover, the more complex one's emotional nature, and the greater the development of the higher forms of feeling, the more intense is the struggle of deliberation or the fight of the desires.

We see, in Halleck's definition, that desire has not only the object of "bringing pleasure or getting rid of pain" for the individual, but that the additional element of the welfare of "some one in whom he is interested" is added, which element is often the deciding factor. This element, of course, arises from the development and cultivation of one's emotional nature. In the same way we also see that it is not merely the *immediate* welfare of one's self or those in whom one is interested that speaks before the bar, but also the more *remote* welfare. This consideration of future welfare depends upon the intellect and cultivated imagination under its control. Moreover, the trained intellect is able to discover possible greater satisfaction in some course of action other than in the one prompted by the clamoring desire of the moment. This explains why the judgment and action of an intelligent man, as a rule, are far different from those of the unintelligent one; and also why a man of culture tends toward different action from that of the uncultured; and likewise, why the man of broad sympathies and high ideals acts in a different way from one of the opposite type. But the principle is ever the same—the feelings manifest in desire, the greatest ultimate satisfaction apparent at the moment is sought, and the strongest set of desires wins the day.

Halleck's comment on this point is interesting. He says: "Desire is not always proportional to the idea of one's own selfish pleasure. Many persons, after forming an idea of the vast amount of earthly distress, desire to relieve it, and the desire goes out in action, as the benevolent societies in every city testify. Here the individual pleasure is none the less, but it is secondary, coming from the pleasure of others. The desire of the *near* often raises a stronger desire than the *remote*. A child frequently prefers a thing immediately if it is only one tenth as good as something he might have a year hence. A student often desires more the leisure of to-day than the success of future years. Though admonished to study, he wastes his time and thus loses incomparably greater future pleasure when he is tossed to the rear in the struggle for existence."

The result of this weighing and balancing of the desire is, or should be, *decision and choice*, which then passes into action. But many persons seem unable to "make up their own mind," and require a push or urge from without before they will act. Others decide, without proper use of the intellect, upon what they call "impulse," but which is merely impatience. Some are like the fabled donkey which starved to death when placed at an equal distance between two equally attractive haystacks and was unable to decide towards which to move. Others follow the example of Jeppe, in the comedy, who, when given a coin with which to buy a piece of soap for his wife, stood on the corner deliberating whether to obey orders or to buy a drink with the money. He wants the drink, but realizes that his wife will beat him if he returns without the soap. "My stomach says drink; my back says soap," says Jeppe. "But," finally he remarks, "is not a man's stomach more to him than his back? Yes, says I."

The final decision depends upon the striking a balance between the desires,—the weighing of desire for and desire against,—desire for this and desire for something else. The strength of the several desires depends upon nearness and present interest arising from attention, as applied to the feelings and emotions arising from heredity, environment, experience, and education, which constitute character; and also upon the degree of intellectual clearness and power in forming correct judgments between the desires.

It must be remembered, however, that the intellect appears not as an opponent of the principle of the satisfaction of desire, but merely as an instrument of the ego in determining which course of action will result in the greatest ultimate satisfaction, direct or indirect, present or future. For, *at the last, every individual acts so as to bring himself the greatest satisfaction, immediate or future, direct or indirect, either personal or through the welfare of others, as this may appear to him at the particular moment of deliberation.* We always act in the direction of that which will greater "content our spirit." This will be found to be the spirit of all decisions, although the motive is often hidden and difficult to find even by the individual himself, many of the strongest motives having their origin in the subconscious planes of mentality.

(3). Action.

The third and final phase of will is that known as action—the act of volition by which the desire-idea is expressed in physical or mental activity. The old conception of the will held that the decisive phase of the will was its characteristic and final phase, ignoring the fact that the very essence or spirit of will is bound up with *action*. Even those familiar with the newer conception frequently assume that the act of decision is the final phase of will, ignoring the fact that we frequently *decide* to do a thing and yet may never carry out the intention and decision. The act of willing is not complete unless action is expressed. There must be the manifestation of the motor element or phase of will, else the will process is incomplete.

A weakness of this last phase of will affects the entire will and renders its processes ineffective. The world is filled with persons who are able to *decide* what is best to do, and what should be done, but who never actually *act* upon the decision. The few persons who promptly follow up the decision with vigorous action are those who accomplish the world's work. Without the full manifestation of this third phase of will the other two phases are useless.

Types of Will

So far we have considered merely the highest type of will—that which is accompanied by conscious deliberation, in which the intellect takes an active part. In this process, not only do the conflicting feelings push themselves forward with opposing claims for recognition, but the intellect is active in examining the case and offering valuable testimony as to the comparative merits of the various claimants and the effect of certain courses of action upon the individual. There are, however, several lower forms of will manifestation which we should briefly consider in passing.

Reflex Action.—The will is moved to action by the reflex activities of the nervous system which have been mentioned in the earlier chapters of this book. In this general type we find unconscious reflex action, such as that manifested when a sleeper is touched and moves away, or when the frog's leg twitches when the nerve end is excited. We also find conscious reflex action, such as that manifested by the winking of the eye, or the performance of habitual physical motion, such as the movement in walking, operating the sewing machine or typewriter, playing the piano, etc.

Impulsive Action.—The will is often moved to action by a dim idea or faint perception of purpose or impulse. The action is almost instinctive, although there is a vague perception of purpose. For instance, we feel an impulse to turn toward the source of a strange sound or sight, or other source of interest or curiosity. Or we may feel an impulse arising from the subconscious plane of our mind, causing a dimly-conscious idea of movement or action to relieve the tension. For instance, one may feel a desire to exercise, or to seek fresh air or green fields, although he had not been thinking of these things at the time. These impulses arise from a subconscious feeling of fatigue or desire for change, which, added to a fleeting idea, produces the impulse. Unless an impulse is inhibited by the will activities inspired by other desires, habits, ideas, or ideals, we act upon it in precisely the same way that a young child or animal does. Hoffding says of this type of action: "The psychological condition of the impulse is, that with the momentary feeling and sensation should be combined a more or less clear idea of something which may augment the pleasure or diminish the pain of the moment."

Instinctive Action.—The will is frequently moved to action by an instinctive stimulus. This form of will activity closely resembles the last mentioned form, and often it is impossible to distinguish between the two. The activities of the bee in building its comb and storing its honey, the work of the silkworm and caterpillar in building their resting places, are examples of this form of action. Indeed, even the building of the nest of the bird may be so classed. In these cases there is an intelligent action toward a definite end, but the animal is unconscious of that end. The experiences of the remote ancestors of these creatures recorded their impressions upon the subconscious mind of the species, and they are transmitted in some way to all of that species. The nervous system of every living thing is a record cylinder of the experiences of its early ancestors, and these cylinders tend to reproduce these impressions upon appropriate occasions. In preceding chapters we have shown that even man is under the influence of instinct to a greater extent than he imagines himself to be.

30
Will-Training

IT is of the utmost importance that the individual develop, cultivate, and train his will so as to bring it under the influence of the higher part of his mental and moral being. While the will is used most effectively in developing and training the intellect and building character, it itself must be trained by itself to habitually come under the guidance of the intellect and under the influence of that which we call character.

The influence of the trained will upon the several mental faculties is most marked. There are no faculties which may not be cultivated by the will. The first and great task of the will in this direction is the control and direction of the attention. The will determines the kind of interest that shall prevail at the moment, and the kind of interest largely determines the character of the man, his tastes, his feelings, his thoughts, his acts. Gordy says: "Coöperating with a pre-existing influence, the will can make a weaker one prevail over a stronger.

* * *

It determines which of pre-existing influences shall have control over the mind."

Moreover, concentrated and continued attention depends entirely upon the exercise of the will. As Gordy says: "If the will relaxes its hold upon the activities of the mind, the attention is liable to be carried away by any one of the thousands of ideas that the laws of association are constantly bringing into our minds."

Even in the matter of mental images the will asserts its sway, and the imagination may be trained to be the obedient servant of the developed will. Regarding the influence of the will upon character, Davidson says: "It is not enough for a man to understand correctly and love duly the conditions of moral life in his own time; he must, still further, be willing and able to fulfill these conditions. And he certainly cannot do this unless his will is trained to perfect freedom, so that it responds, with the utmost readiness, to the suggestions of his discriminating intelligence and the movements of his chastened affections." Halleck says: "We gradually make our characters by separate acts of will, just as a blacksmith by repeated blows beats out a horseshoe or an anchor from a shapeless mass of iron. A finished anchor or horseshoe was never the product of a single blow."

Training the Will

Perhaps the best way to train the will is to *use* it intelligently, and with a purpose. The training of any faculty of the mind is at the same time a training of the will. The attention being so closely allied to the will, it follows that a careful training of attention will result in a strengthening of the will. The training of the emotional side of one's nature also brings results in the strengthening of the will.

Halleck gives his students excellent advice regarding the training of the will. It would be hard to find anything better along these lines than the following from his pen: "Nothing schools the will, and renders it ready for effort in this complex world, better than accustoming it to face disagreeable things. Professor James advises all to do something occasionally for no other reason than that they would rather not do it, if it is nothing more than giving up a seat in a street car. He likens such effort to the insurance that a man pays on his house. He has something that he can fall back on in time of trouble. A will schooled in this way is always ready to respond, no matter how great the emergency. While another would be crying over spilled milk, the possessor of such a will has already found another cow.

* * *

The only way to secure such a will is to practice doing disagreeable things. There are daily opportunities.

* * *

A man who had declared his aversion to what he deemed the dry facts of political economy was one day found knitting his brow over a chapter of John Stuart Mill. When a friend expressed surprise, the man replied: 'I am playing the schoolmaster with myself. I am reading this because I dislike it.' Such a man has the elements of success in him.

* * *

On the other hand, the one who habitually avoids disagreeable action is training his will to be of no use to him at a time when supreme effort is demanded. Such a will can never elbow its way to the front in life."

Habits

Habits are the beaten track over which the will travels. The beaten path of habit is the line of least resistance to the will. One who would train his will must needs pay attention to providing it with the proper mental paths over which to travel. The rule for the creation of habits is simply this: *Travel over the mental path as often as possible*. The rule for breaking undesirable habits is this: *Cultivate the opposite habit*. In these two rules is expressed the gist of what has been written on the subject.

Professor William James has left to the world some invaluable advice regarding the cultivation of right habits. He bases his rules upon those of Professor Bain, elaborates these, and adds some equally good ones. We herewith quote freely from both James and Bain on this subject; it is the best ever written regarding habit building.

I. "In the acquisition of a new habit, or the leaving off of an old one, launch yourself with as strong and decided an initiative as possible. This will give your new beginning such a momentum that the temptation to break down will not occur as soon as it otherwise might; and every day during which a breakdown is postponed adds to the chances of it not occurring at all."—*James.*

II. "Never suffer an exception to occur till the new habit is securely rooted in your life. Every lapse is like the letting fall of a ball of string which one is carefully winding up—a single slip undoes more than a great many turns will wind again."—*James.* "It is necessary, above all things, in such a situation, never to lose a battle. Every gain on the wrong side undoes the effect of many conquests on the right. The essential precaution is so to regulate the two opposing powers that the one may have a series of uninterrupted successes, until repetition has fortified it to such a degree as to enable it to cope with the opposition, under any circumstances."—*Bain.*

III. "Seize the very first possible opportunity to act on every resolution you make, and on every emotional prompting you may experience in the direction of the habits you aspire to gain. It is not in the moment of their forming, but in the moment of their producing *motor effects*, that resolves and aspirations communicate their new 'set' to the brain."—*James.* "The actual presence of the practical opportunity alone furnishes the fulcrum upon which the lever can rest, by which the moral will may multiply its strength and raise itself aloft. He who has no solid ground to press against will never get beyond the stage of empty gesture making."—*Bain.*

IV. "Keep the faculty alive in you by a little gratuitous exercise every day. That is, be systematically ascetic or heroic in little, unnecessary points; do every day something for no other reason than that you would rather not do it, so that when the hour of dire need draws nigh, it may find you not unnerved and untrained to stand the test.

* * *

The man who has daily inured himself to habits of concentrated attention, energetic volition, and self-denial in unnecessary things will stand like a tower when everything rocks around him, and when his softer fellow mortals are winnowed like chaff in the blast."—*James.*

31

Will-Tonic

IN addition to the general rules for developing and training the will given in the preceding chapter, we ask you to tone up and strengthen the will by the inspiration to be derived from the words of some of the world's great thinkers and doers. In these words there is such a vital statement of the recognition, realization, and manifestation of that something within, which we call "will," that it is a dull soul, indeed, which is not inspired by the contagion of the idea. These expressions are the milestones on the Path of Attainment, placed by those who have preceded us on the journey. We submit these quotations without comment; they speak for themselves.

Words of the Wise

"They can who think they can. Character is a perfectly educated will."

"Nothing can resist the will of a man who knows what is true and wills what is good."

"In all difficulties advance and will, for within you is a power, a living force, which the more you trust and learn to use will annihilate the opposition of matter."

"The star of the unconquered will,
It rises in my breast,
Serene and resolute and still,
And calm and self-possessed.
"So nigh is grandeur to our dust,
So near is God to man,
When duty whispers low, 'Thou must!'
The youth replies, 'I can!'"

"The longer I live, the more certain I am that the great difference between men, between the feeble and the powerful, the great and the insignificant, is energy,—invincible determination,—a purpose once fixed, and then death or victory. That quality will do anything that can be done in this world, and no talents, no circumstances, no opportunities will make a two-legged creature a man without it."—*Buxton.*

"The human will, that force unseen,
The offspring of a deathless soul,
Can hew a way to any goal,
Though walls of granite intervene.
"You will be what you will to be;
Let failure find its false content
In that poor word environment,
But spirit scorns it and is free.
"It masters time, it conquers space,
It cows that boastful trickster, chance,
And bids the tyrant circumstance
Uncrown and fill a servant's place."

"Resolve is what makes a man manifest; not puny resolve, not crude determinations, not errant purpose, but that strong and indefatigable will which treads down difficulties and danger as a boy treads down the heaving frost lands of winter, which kindles his eye and brain with a proud pulse beat toward the unattainable. Will makes men giants."—*Donald G. Mitchell.*

"There is no chance, no destiny, no fate
Can circumvent, or hinder, or control
The firm resolve of a determined soul.
Gifts count for nothing, will alone is great;
All things give way before it soon or late.
What obstacle can stay the mighty force
Of the sea-seeking river in its course,
Or cause the ascending orb of day to wait?
Each well-born soul must win what it deserves.
Let the fools prate of luck. The fortunate
Is he whose earnest purpose never swerves,
Whose slightest action, or inaction,
Serves the one great aim. Why, even death itself
Stands still and waits an hour sometimes
For such a will."

—Ella Wheeler Wilcox.

"I have brought myself by long meditation to the conviction that a human being with a settled purpose must accomplish it, and that nothing can resist a will which will stake even existence upon its fulfillment."—*Lord Beaconsfield.*

"A passionate desire and an unwearied will can perform impossibilities, or what may seem to be such to the cold and feeble."—*Sir John Simpson.*

"It is wonderful how even the casualties of life seem to bow to a spirit that will not bow to them, and yield to subserve a design which they may, in their first apparent tendency, threaten to frustrate. When a firm, decisive spirit is recognized, it is curious to see how the space clears around a man and leaves him room and freedom."—*John Foster.*

"The great thing about General Grant is cool persistency of purpose. He is not easily excited, and he has got the grip of a bulldog. When he once gets his teeth in, nothing can shake him off."—*Abraham Lincoln.*

"I am bigger than anything that can happen to me. All these things are outside my door, *and I've got the key*.

* * *

Man was meant to be, and ought to be, stronger and more than anything that can happen to him. Circumstances, 'Fate,' 'Luck,' are all outside; and if he cannot change them, he can always *beat* them."—*Charles F. Lummis.*

"The truest wisdom is a resolute determination."

"Impossible is a word found only in the dictionary of fools."

"Circumstances! I *make* circumstances!"—*Napoleon.*

"He who fails only half wills."—*Suwarrow.*

"That which the easiest becomes a habit in us is the will. Learn, then, to will strongly and decisively; thus fix your floating life, and leave it no longer to be carried hither and thither, like a withered leaf, by every wind that blows."

"Man owes his growth chiefly to that active striving of the will,—that encounter which we call effort,—and it is astonishing to find how often results apparently impracticable are thus made possible.

* * *

It is will—force of purpose—that enables a man to do or be whatever he sets his mind upon being or doing."

"A strong, defiant purpose is many-handed and lays hold of whatever is near that can serve it; it has a magnetic purpose that draws to itself whatever is kindred.

* * *

Let it be your first study to teach the world that you are not wood and straw; that there is some iron in you."—*Munger.*

"It's dogged as does it."—Yorkshire Proverb.

"One talent with a will behind it will accomplish more than ten without it, as a thimbleful of powder in a rifle, the bore of whose barrel will give it direction, will do greater execution than a carload burned in the open air."—*O.S. Marden.*

"Will may not endow man with talents or capacities; but it does one very important matter—it enables him to make the best, the very best, of his powers."—*Fothergill.*

"Tender-handed stroke a nettle,
And it stings you for your pains.
Grasp it like a man of mettle,
And it soft as down remains."

"Don't flinch; don't foul; but hit the line hard."—*Roosevelt.*

"The more difficulties one has to encounter, within and without, the more significant and the higher in inspiration his life will be."